Post-Project Reviews
to Gain Effective
Lessons Learned

Post-Project Reviews to Gain Effective Lessons Learned

Project Management Institute

Terry Williams, PhD, PMP

ISBN 13: 978-1-933890-24-1
ISBN 10: 1-933890-24-X

Published by: Project Management Institute, Inc.
                 Four Campus Boulevard
                 Newtown Square, Pennsylvania 19073-3299 USA
                 Phone: +610-356-4600
                 Fax: +610-356-4647
                 E-mail: pmihq@pmi.org
                 Internet: www.pmi.org

PMI Publications welcomes corrections and comments on its books. Please feel free to send comments on typographical, formatting, or other errors. Simply make a copy of the relevant page of the book, mark the error, and send it to: Book Editor, PMI Publications, Four Campus Boulevard, Newtown Square, PA 19073-3299 USA.

PMI books are available at special quantity discounts to use as premiums and sales promotions, or for use in corporate training programs, as well as other educational programs. For more information, please write to Bookstore Administrator, PMI Publications, Four Campus Boulevard, Newtown Square, PA 19073-3299 USA, or e-mail: booksonline@pmi.org. Or contact your local bookstore.

The paper used in this book complies with the Permanent Paper Standard issued by the National Information Standards Organization (Z39.48—1984).

10 9 8 7 6 5 4 3 2 1

CONTENTS

1
INTRODUCTION

1.1 Introduction

The need to manage projects well, and to learn from one project to the next, is of vital importance as our world becomes more and more project-based. Our management of complex projects is often seen as less effective than it might be, and consequently, we do need to learn from one project to the next. This is a well-known theory (Collison and Parcell 2001; Kerzner 2000)—but in practice, projects are often not reviewed at all for various reasons (Williams et al. 2001) If they are reviewed, the methods don't account for the complexity or try to explain causality, so there is no understanding about what went wrong (or right) and why (MacMaster 2000). So with a few exceptions, it appears that project reviews are infrequently performed and useful lessons are not captured. If we did gain lessons, these need to be incorporated into the processes and policies of our organizations; a "lessons learned" process needs to be implemented and then reflected upon to produce double-loop learning. The need to consider what is best practice in reviewing projects is evident.

At the end of 2004, while working at Strathclyde University, Glasgow, Scotland, UK, I responded to a request for research proposals from the Project Management Institute (PMI®), Newtown Square, PA, USA, with a proposal to look into post-project reviews, and PMI awarded me a research grant. In the middle of the contract, I moved to Southampton University, UK (also Concertante Consulting, London, UK) and the work was completed there.

The objectives of the research include identifying current practice as well as practice currently considered best practice for lessons learned in the project management field, and comparing current practices with advances in understanding and modeling of project behavior to identify project lessons not being learned. This work sought to answer the following research questions which are of different types; therefore, different methodological approaches were required as is often the case with good management research (Easterby-Smith, Thorpe, and Lowe 1991).

1. *Research Question 1 (RQ1)* comprised two questions: "What is current practice?" and "What is currently considered best practice?" These are factual questions that are best explored using positivist techniques. A literature survey (Activity 1) and questionnaire (Activity 2) were used to investigate this.

2. *Research Question 2 (RQ2)* asked "Do these techniques actually achieve their purpose?" and is harder to answer with an unambiguous positivist answer. A literature survey (Activity 1) and questionnaire (Activity 2) along with interviews to gain subjective opinions (Activity 3), and some phenomenological analyses of an actual case study (Activity 4) were used to investigate whether these cases are indeed establishing the difficult-to-identify lessons.

3. *Research Question 3 (RQ3)* asked "Can we identify practical techniques to help draw out the difficult lessons from the projects?" is a practical question, and was approached by using the knowledge from Activities 1 through 3 and drawing out the experience of Activity 4, along the lines of Mode II research common in top-quality UK management research (Starkey and Madan 2001).

4. *Research Question 4 (RQ4)* asked "How can such lessons be incorporated into organizational practice?" Although a short research project, this is again a practical question, which will be approached by considering the literature (Activity 1), looking at actual practices (Activity 2), and considering both by interviews (Activity 3) and observations (Activity 4) as to how and whether lessons are taken into organizational procedures.

The program thus consisted of four main activities. The first pair of activities established the current state of practice:

-   *Activity 1* carried out a survey of literature relevant to learning lessons in projects.

-   *Activity 2* surveyed the current practice of establishing and recording "lessons learned" throughout the project management community using an online questionnaire survey.

The second pair of activities, which formed the considerably smaller part of the study, looked at some particular examples:

-   *Activity 3* looked more in depth into current practice in six organizations, using semi-structured interviews.

-   *Activity 4* looked at a particular organization, and a particular project within that organization, to see how lessons are learned and how they can be learned.

I led the research work. A significant part of the work for Activities 1 and 2 was carried out by Judith Stark (also of Strathclyde University, Glasgow, Scotland, UK). For Activity 1, there was some additional help with literature.

This research report on the work is divided into six chapters. After this introduction, Chapters 2 through 4 correspond to Activities 1–4; Chapter 2 covers the literature survey; Chapter 3 covers the online survey; Chapter 4 describes the interviews; and Chapter 5 reviews the case study. Chapter 6 provides some brief conclusions. Chapters 2–5 are designed to be self-standing and each can be read on their own.

2
LITERATURE SURVEY

2.1 Introduction

This chapter describes the results of the survey of literature on the use of "lessons learned" from projects. The report was based on a Procite© database, which included not only references but a categorization by the keywords given in Table 2-1. The database included 280 records, of which 243 documents had been read fully and are discussed in the following paragraphs. For 28 references, only summaries, abstracts, or book reviews were studied or are included because they are referenced by one of the 243 documents; and another 9 appeared relevant but were not found sufficiently appropriate for inclusion when the literature survey was written up and therefore do not appear here. Due to the tremendous number of documents, this survey should be considered as a summary rather than a full exploration of the literature.

The survey was wide-ranging and sought views beyond the project-management literature. Databases (including *Google scholar)* were used with relevant keywords. Key papers were selected and "forward chaining" was performed (i.e., searching citation indexes for papers that refer to these papers). Some particularly relevant journals were checked in their entirety for the previous 10 years, namely:

* *Construction Management and Economics*
* *IEEE Transactions on Engineering Management*
* *International Journal of Project Management*
* *Management Learning* (only from Vol 29 [March 1998] to present)
* *Organization Science*
* *Project Management Journal*
* *The Learning Organization*

In addition, some conferences were checked in their entirety, namely:

- PMI full conferences 2001–2003

- PMI Research Conferences 2000–2004

- IPMA conferences 1996–2004

- IRNOP (International Research Network on Organizing by Projects) conferences 2002-2004

- PMI Europe conferences 2000–2001

The *Index of PMI Periodical Publications: 1996–2002*, supplied by PMI, was also studied.

The topic of lessons learned can be regarded as very narrow or very broad. Clearly, it is important to gain the theoretical underpinnings of the how-to-learn lessons, and this means going beyond reports of implementations of project learning. However, the review of the entire organizational learning and knowledge management literatures was outside of the scope of this study; therefore, this survey contains only articles particularly relevant to project learning or fundamental articles or review articles of state-of-the-art theory. For those who want to read further about the literature on learning, DeFillippi (2001) gives an overview on different perspectives of learning from projects and where to find more about them, covering: *(a)* action learning (Revans, Smith)—people learn by working on real problems; *(b)* action science (Argyris and Schon)—project participants reflect on theories in use with the help of a facilitator; *(c)* action research (Lewin)—combines theory building with research on practical problems; *(d)* communities of practice (Wenger, Brown, and Duguid)—learning occurs naturally through communities, with the deepest learning occurring when people's positions move within a community and at the intersections of multiple communities; and *(e)* reflective practice (Raelin). Much of this will be touched upon as part of this book.

The problem of how to learn from projects has long been an issue with project-based organizations, and this book will discuss some of the reasons why. Almost forty years ago, Middleton (1967) identified this as a problem with project-based organizations as opposed to functional ones: "Lessons learned on one project may not be communicated to other projects. One executive who was transferring from a project being phased out to a new project found the same mistakes being made that he had encountered on his former assignment three years earlier. He felt that the problem resulted from splitting normal functional responsibilities among project organizations and from not having enough qualified, experienced employees to spread among all organizations." Although our views of projects might be different today, Packendorff (1995), a leader in the Scandinavian school looking at projects as organizations rather than tools and seeking to go beyond normative statements, said "theories on learning in projects . . . are almost non-existent today." This is despite a clear recognition, as Sense (2002) points out, that projects offer enormous potential for learning even though this is neglected in traditional project management practice.

Learning clearly always happens to some extent by the nature of undertaking projects. Schofield and Wilson (1995), for example, looked at capital projects within the UK National Health Service and observed that learning did happen (in three ways: termed mechanical, cognitive, and behavioral) but they concluded "none of the team set about achieving organizational learning in a premeditated way." In this book, we are looking towards the more systematic collection and distribution of lessons from projects. Ayas (1998) said that "learning within a project does not happen naturally; it is a complex process that needs to be managed. It requires deliberate attention, commitment, and continuous investment of resources" (cited in Sense 2003a).

This document is restricted to learning about project processes or how to manage and execute projects. It is not aimed towards learning technical knowledge from projects (such as in work along the lines of Nobeoka 1995)—it is about the project-management process rather than the content of projects.

Case studies	Case studies of companies that use lessons learned
Communities of practice (general)	General papers about communities of practice or similar networks
Communities of practice (projects)	Papers about communities of practice or similar networks where the issues are specific to projects and related to process rather than content
Facilitating factors and hindrances	Factors which facilitate or hinder collecting lessons or distributing lessons
General personal learning	General material about the way people learn
Introduction	A few papers referred to in Section 2.1 of this book
Knowledge management (general)	Papers about how lessons are transferred throughout the organization
Knowledge management (projects)	Papers about how lessons about projects (related to process rather than content) are transferred throughout the organization
Motivation	The benefits of learning from projects
Narratives	Reporting from projects by narratives
Nature of knowledge	General material about knowledge
Organizational learning (general)	How organizations learn
Organizational learning (projects)	How organizations learn from projects
Practices (group)	Specific practices used by groups / organizations
Practices (individual)	Specific practices used by individuals
Prevalence	Evidence of how prevalent lessons learned activity is
Standards and maturity models	Standards and maturity models related to lessons learned
Systemicity general	Complex systemic effects in projects
Systemicity in project lessons	Complex systemic effects in projects and how they impact lessons learned

Table 2-1 **Keywords used in database**

We will not be considering cases of particular projects that have gone wrong (e.g., Glass 1998) and trying to analyze them; rather, we will be looking at the literature to learn how organizations learn lessons from projects they have undertaken.

The structure of this document is as follows. Following this introduction, we shall look at:

- *Motivation:* why look at learning from projects?

- *Basic concepts:* what is knowledge? And what is learning?

- *The current situation:* what do project-management and other standards say about learning lessons? How prevalent actually are such practices?

- *Creating knowledge:* techniques, the use of narratives, dealing with systemicity, and factors that facilitate or hinder creating knowledge from projects.

- *Transferring knowledge:* organizational learning and knowledge management in projects, practices for distributing lessons, factors that facilitate or hinder distributing lessons from projects, and one particular idea, that of "communities of practice."

- *Case studies:* a brief mention of some case studies.

- *Conclusions:* finally, some conclusions.

2.2 **Motivation**

It might be thought that it goes without saying that learning from one project to another is a worthwhile aim, upon which it is worth expending effort. Abramovici (1999) for example tells us that "lessons learned" is a good thing to do, while outlining some basic practices. Similarly, Pinto (1999) states that information systems projects have a poor success record, describes evidence supporting this and reasons for it, then goes on to stress the need to pass lessons learned downstream through post-project review meetings. In the field of complex product systems, Davies and Brady (2000) demonstrate the learning cycle of such projects, which requires a step: "lessons learned from the project and recommendations for improvements can be transferred to current or succeeding projects." Kerzner (2000) places continuous learning and improvement as the highest level of project management maturity in an organization, and states that "without 'discounted' lessons learned, a company can quickly revert from maturity to immaturity in project management. Knowledge is lost and past mistakes are repeated." Berke (2001) says that "Organizational learning and organizational knowledge make up the CIQ [corporate intelligence quotient] . . . Best practices and lessons learned are the building blocks of organizational learning and organizational knowledge."

Why is learning lessons important? And is there evidence that it gives some use? This section provides a few sources that support the motivation to carry out lessons learned activities.

There are fundamental aspects of the nature of project-based organizations that require concentration on learning. Projects are, by nature, temporary organizations, and any learning that is accumulated in a project will largely dissipate at the end of the project unless attention is paid to the collection and dissemination of that knowledge. This has become increasingly recognized as the nature of projects as temporary organizations have been studied, particularly in the Scandinavian project management school. Ekstedt et al. (1999), for example, discuss the central importance of "knowledge formation" (by which they mean the combination of learning and embedding that learning): *(a)* they say that permanent organizations, which have a long-term perspective, generally have mechanisms that are built in for learning, but the new project-intensive organizational structures (i.e., "temporary organizations") are action- and task-oriented and not geared for learning; and *(b)* individuals become more able and experienced, but there is often no mechanism or motivation for that learning to be shared within the company. They claim that "in temporary organizations . . . the most important thing in the design of a project is the combination of project members and the resources allotted to the project that is relying on the combinatorics of different stocks of knowledge"; however, "the outcomes of the knowledge processes that take place are difficult to feed back to the permanent organization." Brady, Marshall, Prencipe, and Tell (2002) describe a number of barriers to learning from projects, in particular the absence of departmentally held "knowledge silos"; the uniqueness of projects, with long life cycles, so a long time interval elapses before lessons are retrieved; and their temporary nature, requiring new "human encounters" for each project. Similarly, Disterer (2002) looks at the need to manage the retention of knowledge because of the fragmentation of the organization into project teams, concluding: "only a few firms manage systematically to identify and transfer valuable knowledge from projects to following projects." Bresnen, Goussevskaia, and Swan (2004) discuss the contradiction between short-term aims of projects and long-term aim of organizational learning, showing that knowledge management will depend on the degree of projectization of the firm (pure project firms will be different from matrix, and these will be different from functional organizations that only do occasional projects).

Project processes are generally temporary and unique, with non-routine features. Gann and Salter (2000) say that a particular challenge for project-based firms is to integrate their project and business processes, so the experiences of projects need to be integrated into the business processes, and knowledge acquired from projects needs to flow back to the core resources of the firm. Brady, Marshall, Prencipe, and Tell (2002) describe a further number of characteristics of projects, which contribute to the difficulties of learning, including customization (either because previous solutions are obsolete or are being driven by customer demands), discontinuity (both temporal and organizational; project work is highly discontinuous, with a narrow focus and task oriented), complexity, interdependence (systemic, so it is not always possible to rely on past experience to solve current problems), and uncertainty. However, that is not to say that all projects are completely different—and the "misguided belief" that they inhibit learning (Cooper, Lyneis, and Bryant 2002).

Furthermore, projects not only cross organizational functions, they are trans-disciplinary, so even beyond the project management literature, Gibbons et al. (1994) have explored changes in the manner in which knowledge is produced. They discuss the change in "mode of knowledge production" by contrasting the traditional mode in which discipline-based (academic) institutions define a problem and use these institutions to develop knowledge and maintain quality control, with a new mode in which knowledge is produced in the context of application, knowledge is transdisciplinary, and knowledge production has to be socially accountable. So we need new mechanisms to capture and disseminate knowledge beyond the traditional disciplinary and functional structures.

Cooke-Davies (2002) describes a major ongoing empirical study, and in this paper identified 12 key success factors in project-oriented organizations; one of these is "an effective means of learning from experience." Menke (1997) describes a study of 79 R&D companies and gives 10 "best practices'" for R&D decisions which confer R&D competitive advantage. Once again, "learn from post-project audits" is one of the 10 best practices, although it is worth noting that it comes in as the lowest when measured by frequency of use (in this survey, in only 24% of companies). Kotnour's (2000) influential survey of 43 project managers within the Project Management Institute, based on *subjective* measures, indicates that project management performance is associated with project knowledge; project management knowledge is supported by project learning activities; the level of activity of producing lessons learned is related to inter-project learning; and that "learning support" (for example, collecting data and having appropriate corporate culture about learning lessons) is needed for all learning activities.

The literature provides a number of reasons for, or perceived benefits from, managing the learning from projects. These include

- Project managers learn how to manage experientially, and it is important to reflect and gain these lessons. "Research shows that the majority (85%) of project personnel have gained their knowledge, both explicit and tacit, through experiential learning" (Turner, Keegan, and Crawford 2000).

- Learning lessons from projects can feed into the project assessment, risk analysis, or initial planning of the next project. Neale and Holmes (1990) describe a survey of finance directors in 1,000 companies regarding post-auditing procedures for capital projects, so the emphasis was on improving decisions about whether to invest in a project, for example better proposals, better evaluation, and better financial control: 38% of the survey identified "encouraging more realistic project assessments" as the main aim of post-project auditing and 30% identified "encouraging greater realism in project appraisal" as a main benefit; they conclude that post-auditing can "radically improve the quality of investment decision-making." Williams (2005) describes an extensive case study in which a number of lessons learned were used as feedback to the formal risk management pre-project process of a large corporation.

* In general, lessons are used to feed into improving project-management processes—the primary reason for carrying out post-audits, according to Azzone and Maccarrone's (2001) survey of 124 Italian firms (albeit with only 34 responses).

* Similarly, lessons are used to improve management decision-making, which is identified as the second reason in Azzone and Maccarrone's (2001) survey, and as a main benefit by 26% of the respondents in Neale and Holmes' (1990) survey.

* Projects are part of a cycle and lessons learned can be tested and experimented with during the next generation of the cycle. Kotnour (1999), for example, presents learning from projects as a plan-do-study-act cycle (adapted from quality management), occurring both intra- and inter-project, where the "act" is making use of the lessons learned in future projects. He views learning cycles as an inherent part of the project and series of projects, not just a separate activity at the end (an empirical study of 43 project managers showed this is how they view learning), and indeed "every step in the project management process, if viewed from the learning perspective, can serve as the basis for producing and sharing knowledge for the project team."

* Lessons learned procedures are important to disseminate knowledge within the project team, beyond the team to other projects, and even to other organizations. Busby's (1999a) study of post-project review meetings highlighted one main strength as disseminating knowledge within the project team and promoting remedies; dissemination to other projects was also mentioned. Going beyond the project team, Gulliver (1987) describes the influential post project appraisal (PPA) unit within British Petroleum, with two key elements being *(a)* its independence and *(b)* the fact that PPA is company-wide so projects can be reviewed and lessons passed on to project teams elsewhere in the world. Holt, Love, and Li (2000) describe how learning underlies inter-company alliances: being able to learn collectively.

* Lessons learned are useful for benchmarking. Garnett and Pickrell (2000) describe some action research developing a methodology for benchmarking in the construction industry, noting that much of the benefit was derived from generating and sharing ideas in the interactive activity (a social constructivist view) rather than fact finding about hard measures (positivist). (Note that the idea of project benchmarking [Ottmann 2000], for example, learning from others' projects is a different topic.)

- Post-project audits to capture lessons learned can also have the side-benefit for senior management of being able to check on the performance of their personnel (Azzone and Maccarrone's [2001] third reason) or on their project managers' expertise (the main aim for 22% in Neale and Holmes' [1990] survey).

- Kumar and Terpstra (2004) note the key role that a post-mortem can play at the stage-gates of the new product development process, as lessons learned in one (usually less costly) phase can feed through to the next phase.

However, Learning lessons and disseminating the knowledge gained from them is not simple. Barnes and Wearne (1993) in their look into the following 25 years of project management said "A problem which may well continue is that of presenting the lessons of the completed projects . . . in a form which is brief enough to attract busy people . . . yet is specific enough to persuade them." Two particular issues in the exercise need particular attention to make the lessons useful:

- The need to gain depth in the lessons rather than obvious or simple lessons. Busby's (1999a) survey identified one limitation of the reviews he studied as shallow diagnosis, he claimed because of *(a)* a preference for causal rather than diagnostic reasoning (diagnostic learning is harder to do and involves more blame, which is socially awkward but leads to deeper diagnosis), *(b)* not enough "why," *(c)* a norm of constructive criticism inhibits criticism with no immediate solutions. This highlights the main issue—the need to look into the systemic reasons for project outcomes—which we will look at further in Section 2.5.3; the issue is highlighted in the case study in Williams (2005).

- Secondly, there is the need to gain generalizable lessons rather than lessons specific to that one project (see Toft's [1992] distinction between organization-specific learning and isomorphic learning [universally applicable lessons gained from analysis of factors]). Lack of generalization was another main limitation that Busby (1999a) saw in the reviews he studied. One good example of reviews being used for general experimentation is Cooper, Lyneis, and Bryant (2002), who present their work as a dynamics-based "learning system" for cross-project learning, used by managers to test ideas and see impacts, and to record best practice.

Procedures to learn and disseminate lessons from projects need to be organized. Davies and Brady (2000) claimed in their study of suppliers of Complex Product Systems that "learning tends to be on an ad-hoc basis, with few systematic efforts to spread the initial learning throughout the organization." Ayas (1996) says that "learning within a project does not happen naturally; it is a complex process that needs to be managed. It requires deliberate attention, commitment, and continuous investment of resources . . .

Learning . . . has to be managed together with the project and must be integrated into project management as standard practice." These procedures cannot stand alone: Cavaleri and Fearon (2000) considered that organizational learning is unmanageable if seen as an adjunct to other processes and has to be integrated into core processes; they provide a framework for integrating organizational learning with project management.

Learning is so fundamental to projects that many writers espouse projects particularly as learning mechanisms. Ayas and Zeniuk (2001) discuss promoting projects as learning vehicles and developing communities of practice. Similarly, Sense (2003b) discusses the importance of managing learning in project teams and describes project teams as embryonic communities of practice as they provide an opportunity to learn provided that their focus is shifted to include learning. Arthur, DeFillippi, and Jones (2001) also look at project-based learning, classifying project success by both dimensions of project performance and learning.

Indeed, Bredillet (2004a) claims projects are *the* key learning arena in organizations. Brady and Davies (2004) show how knowledge generated by learning from projects can lead to far-reaching changes in the strategic focus of an organization. Project-led (bottom-up) learning happens in phases: an exploratory "vanguard project" phase, project-to-project (through lessons learned), and project-to-organization, which is fed back to senior management and used to formulate new strategy. As firms advance through the phases, there is a transition from exploration to exploitation, and businesses can plan to move quickly to exploitation (top-down learning).

2.3 Concepts

There are four general concepts that need to be briefly considered before we can look at how people learn from, and increase their knowledge within, projects:

- For an individual, what is knowledge?

- For an individual, what is learning?

- For an organization, what is organizational learning?

- For an organization, what is knowledge management?

2.3.1 Knowledge

The question of what knowledge is has exercised many authors since the time of Aristotle; clearly "knowledge" is not the same as "information" (McDermott 1999). It is not within the scope of this book to cover all of these arguments.

In this matter, however, the work of three authors clearly stands out. The first is Polanyi

(1962), who established the idea of knowledge being internal and personal, or "tacit" and thus not necessarily easy to codify (as opposed to "explicit" knowledge, which can be expressed and shared in highly specified formats). Subsequent work on how people learn and what personal knowledge means is based on his seminal work. However, individuals who learn and keep knowledge to themselves is not sufficient to help organizations learn and develop. As the requirement to help develop "learning organizations" grew, the work of two other seminal authors has been particularly influential. Senge's work (Senge 1990 and Senge et al. 1994) described the "learning organization," and this work will be referred to later. The other particularly influential author (and the second whose work on "knowledge" has been particularly influential) was Nonaka (particularly Nonaka and Takeuchi 1995 but also Nonaka 1991), who described how Japanese companies working in innovation created "knowledge-creating" companies, and whose work requires a careful explication of what is "knowledge." This work includes a model of knowledge creation within the organization based on the interrelationships between tacit and explicit knowledge.

When looking at knowledge as "tacit," "tacit knowledge" is difficult to define and operationalize. Cook and Brown (1999) provide a distinction between explicit and tacit knowledge as follows: explicit knowledge can be spelled out or formalized, and tacit knowledge is that associated with skills or "know-how." Ambrosini and Bowman (2001) look at the definition of tacit knowledge and within the context of the resource-based view of the firm, redefine it as tacit skills; this enables the authors to propose ways in which tacit knowledge can be operationalized, using a methodology incorporating causal mapping, "Self-Q," semi-structured interviews, and the use of metaphors. Johnson, Lorenz, and Lundvall (2002) say that learning (of "tacit" knowledge) is not just about codifying knowledge; when one is deciding whether to codify one needs to take into account: *(a)* the amount that will be lost in the transformation process and *(b)* whether codification is an improvement or not. They recognize that codification can stimulate learning when used to refine models and create shared vocabulary and when used to support the process of "reflection, explication, and documentation of practices." They then make distinctions between four different kinds of knowledge: know-what, know-why, know-how, and know-who.

Isabella's (1990) work looks at the development of knowledge within an organization—particularly relevant to the development of knowledge within projects—as a process of sense-making. Isabella looks at how managers construe events around them and make sense of events in their organization. This will become an important theme later in this section, and also as we explore the ideas in Sections 2.3.2, 2.5.2, and 2.6.1. A key element of knowledge for this study is how *groups* of managers learn rather than individual managers. Knowledge creation is a social process as well as an individual process, sharing tacit knowledge (see von Krogh 1998, based on some ideas of Nonaka and Takeuchi [1995]). Thus our understanding of what knowledge is has to look at the subtle interplay between tacit and explicit, and between individual and group knowledge. Cook and Brown (1999) consider that traditional understanding of the nature of knowledge is based on the "epistemology of possession" as it treats knowledge as something people possess, but that this epistemology cannot account for the knowing found in individual and group practice—so that knowing as action calls for an "epistemology of practice." Cook and Brown claim that the literature tends to treat knowledge as being essentially of one kind and that the epistemology assumed in the literature tends to favor the individual over the group and explicit knowledge instead of tacit knowledge. However, they believe that: "Organizations are better understood if explicit, tacit, individual, and group knowledge are treated as four distinct and coequal forms of knowledge (each doing work the others cannot), and if knowledge and knowing are seen as mutually enabling (and not competing)" [Paper Abstract], and go into detail on these four distinct and coequal forms of knowledge. They also see a distinction between knowledge that is "part of practice" and that knowledge which is "possessed in the head." They refer to the latter as *knowledge* and the former as *knowing*. The focus of the article is more on knowing, and the authors discuss the interplay between the two terms as a way in which new knowledge and new ways of knowing are formed. The authors draw on Dewey's concept of *productive inquiry* in examining the way in which knowledge can be visualized as "a tool at the service of knowing." To help in this exposition, the authors apply their perspective [of seeing distinct forms of knowledge and of viewing knowledge as a tool of knowing] to three cases, which they say "help make clearer some of the actionable and theoretically significant implications of this perspective."

Schulz (2001) also looks at the relationship between the production of knowledge and the flow [vertical or horizontal] of knowledge within organizations. This topic is felt to be important as ". . . each process conceivably depends on the other." The author finds that the production of knowledge in organizational subunits of a firm affects the outflow of knowledge to other units of the same firm: horizontal flows are to peer units and vertical flows are to supervisory units. The author found that "exposure to internal and external sources of newness" and the "uniqueness of experiences" intensify vertical outflows of knowledge, but do not affect horizontal outflows. On the other hand, "reciprocating" and "substitution" affect horizontal outflows but affect vertical outflows much less (the paper includes descriptions of these variables). "It thus appears that collecting new knowledge increases vertical outflows and combining old knowledge intensifies horizontal outflows . . . different kinds of knowledge flow in different directions: New knowledge flows mainly vertically, and incremental knowledge flows mainly horizontally" (p. 674).

Later, we shall return to the way in which knowledge flows within an organization, but it is worth noting that Lesser, Fontaine, and Slusher (2000) explain how organizations are using communities in order to enhance the creation, sharing, and application of knowledge. They highlight people, places, and things as being the three basic components of communities; while IT is also important, the main emphasis is on the social aspects involved in the processes of creating and sharing knowledge.

A key element in understanding the nature of knowledge creation (that is, the manner in which knowledge is made) is the manner in which knowledge is justified. von Krogh and

Grand (1999) "... conceive justification as the permanent corporate and management activity of relating issues and tasks to a generally accepted corporate knowledge base ... [justification] means understanding the mechanisms which decide whether new insights, concepts and ideas are rejected, returned for further elaboration, or finally appropriated as relevant" (p. 16–17). They use the concept of "dominant logic" to try to understand justification.

This discussion pertained to the nature of knowledge in general. Why are these aspects particularly relevant for understanding knowledge within projects? This is because of the following:

- Projects are complex systems, which means that the way in which we organize our thinking about those systems is also complex (Tsoukas and Hatch 2001). They point out that the nature of this complexity affects how we generate knowledge, in particular making narrative types of thinking more appropriate than logico-scientific (i.e., propositional) thinking.

- Real projects are often very much more concerned with sense-making rather than carrying out a full-formed plan, which affects how we can learn from projects (Ivory et al. 2004). Projects frequently take place in a context of confusion, and controversy can help to create new knowledge (Fernie, Green, Weller, and Newcombe 2003).

- Projects are temporary organizations, and there are issues around the lack of time for developing trust in such organizations, which means that knowledge generation and sharing is different from that in permanent organizational structures (Koskinen, Pihlanto, and Vanharanta 2003).

- The whole idea of project management imposes an ontology and a specific way of thinking within a company; this immediately frames ways of thinking when reviewing projects, and can pose difficulties in critically thinking through what really happened (Hodgson 2002).

- We have to learn not just about technical aspects but how our social structures have behaved. For example, Vaughan's (1996) analysis of the Challenger launch decision concluded that the Challenger disaster was not "a technical failure due to managerial wrongdoing and production pressures" (as cited for instance in the U.S. Presidential Commission Reports) but "a mistake embedded in the banality of competition, an unprecedented, uncertain technology, incrementalism, patterns of information, routinization, organizational and interorganizational structures, and a complex culture." The argument is that "mistakes and disasters are socially organized and produced by social structures and culture" (quotes taken from Mitev 1998).

2.3.2 **Learning**

If this is what *knowledge* is, what does *learning* mean within the context of projects? Clearly these are related entities: "Learning and knowledge are intertwined in an iterative, mutually reinforcing process. While learning (the process) produces new knowledge, knowledge impacts future learning" (Vera and Crossan 2003 cited in Scarbrough et al. 2004).

Mumford (1994) says that we need to enable managers to recognize opportunities for learning and learn effectively from experience. He describes four approaches to learning: *(a)* intuitive (no explicit process, not aware of learning happening), *(b)* incidental (reflection following some jolt, e.g., a mishap), *(c)* retrospective (learning by routinely reviewing, not just mishaps), and *(d)* prospective (opportunities to learn are identified in advance). Managers are not shown how to reflect on what has happened or to plan to learn. Some managers are not aware of the benefits of doing so, and this limits the quality of learning they can achieve.

However, clearly reflection plays a key part in this process. Smith (2001) says that "Most of the time we have experiences from which we never learn" and describes the framework and tools for reflective learning in an organization. Winter and Thomas (2004) believe that project management is less about applying specific techniques and more about the powers of managing, which implies that a project manager's education or professional development should focus on developing practitioners' critical awareness and reflective practice. Scarbrough, Swan, and Preston (1999) provide a good review of recent literature on the process of learning by reflection.

Zollo and Winter (2002) describe three types of learning behaviors: tacit accumulation of experience (semiautomatic), knowledge articulation, and knowledge codification (deliberate). They indicate that dynamic capability ("a learned and stable pattern of collective activity through which the organization systematically generates and modifies its operating routines in pursuit of improved effectiveness") arises from the interaction of the three learning behaviors.

As discussed in the previous section, reflection and learning within projects takes place within a team. Learning is not only about acquiring information, but also socialization and requiring appropriate social contexts (Gherardi, Nicolini, and Odella [1998]). Raelin (2001) discusses learning through reflection with others and provides the what, why, and how to do it, claiming this is particularly applicable to learning from projects.

Two names with very particular lines of approach should be noted. The first is Ralph Stacy, whose work on complex responsive processes in organizations shows the importance of socially constructed knowledge creation such as narratives and community of practice. Stacy (2001), for example, outlines Weick's ideas about sense-making and mental models and incorporates them into the structure of complex responsive processes. This work will be important as we develop ideas about knowledge and understanding arising from the complexity of organizations and projects. The second is von Glasersfeld (1995), who can be identified as the key writer in radical constructivism and who stated its basic principles as being that knowledge is not passively received either through the senses or by way of communication but is actively built up by the cognizing subject; and that the function of cognition is adaptive and serves the subject's organization of the experiential world, not the discovery of an objective, ontological reality: "Causality, then, is part of the design that reason imposes on experience to make it understandable" (p. 42); this work will be important as we consider "knowledge" and "knowing" with a suitably critical approach (whatever our own individual ontological or epistemological stance).

Johanssen, Olaisen, and Olsen's (1999) paper clearly explains some of the principles related to learning. For example, the relationship between information and action in the concept of learning: "For most people learning will most likely be synonymous with information acquisition (Machlup)." However, we do not learn by acquiring information. We neither learned how to swim, nor to read or cycle, by acquiring information on swimming, reading, or cycling (Polanyi). There is, in other words, no learning separated from action (Nonaka and Takeuchi). Action is not enough to learn—time has to be built in for reflection relative to the action as well as what is learned (Bandura, Piaget, Rolf). "A major part of learning is then carried out by means of the processes: planning, action, reflection."

2.3.3 **Organizational Learning**

The move from the individual to the organization is not simple. Simon (1991) notes that: "All learning takes place inside individual human heads; an organization learns in only two ways: *(a)* by the learning of its members, or *(b)* by ingesting new members who have knowledge the organization didn't previously have. But . . . what an individual learns in an organization is very much dependent on what is already known to (or believed by) other members of the organization and what kinds of information are present in the organizational environment."

Kim (1993) stresses the importance of making the distinction between the organization and the individual, explicit in the analysis of organizational learning, and develops a model showing the links between individual and organizational learning by means of "shared mental models," what he describes as "the thought constructs that affect how people and organizations operate in the world." Cross and Baird (2000) talk about the need to embed learning within the wider company; they take a proactive stance, targeting learning when it needs to be learned.

As we move from the individual to the organization, we should note the inter-relation between these two: DeFillippi and Arthur (2002) show how workplace learning (knowledge creation and sharing) happens in four contexts: individual, company, community, and industry; and while these are usually studied in isolation, they argue that they are strongly inter-related so it is just as important to understand the connections between them. "Each learning context is a contested domain in which the context and actors operating within the context exert reciprocal influence on each other. It is out of such contested, reciprocal interactions that meaning is constructed and learning arises." Furthermore, for many, the process of reflection and knowledge creation is a social process. Purser, Pasmore, and Tenkasi (1992), for example, looked at *deliberation* in R&D teams and showed that learning for complex project development was enhanced by deliberations. They noted that small informal forums were conducive to knowledge-sharing and active inquiry—by exposing people to the big picture of the overall product system, using a participative decision-making approach. Newell and Huang (2005) use Nonaka's work to look at knowledge creation in multidisciplinary teams, and note the importance of the collaborative nature of teams. Fong (2002) similarly assesses Nonaka and Takeuchi's (1995) knowledge creation model in looking at knowledge creation in multidisciplinary project teams. Fong proposes a model of the processes of knowledge creation within such teams made up of five processes: boundary crossing, knowledge sharing, generation, integration, and collective project learning. Ramaprasad and Prakash (2003) point out that one needs to take local knowledge and integrate it with generic knowledge, and their methods of learning are based on ideas "emerging" from the project, based on concepts such as constructionism and critical thinking. Crossan, Lane, and White (1999) put this into a neat framework as they give what they call "the four I's of organizational learning": intuiting, interpreting, integrating, and institutionalizing, referring to the individual, individual, group, and organization level, respectively.

Spender (1996) tries to pull together the ideas of organizational knowledge, organizational learning, and memory. ". . . The fragmentation of the [organizational learning] literature is the result of the two methodological manoeuvres institutionalized into the contemporary analysis of organizational knowledge. The first separates the notions of knowledge, learning, and memory, presuming each can be treated independently. But we see the three concepts are interdependent parts of a single system of ideas about organizations and their knowledge processes . . . This triangle of interdependency and interdefinition is the foundation on which the rest of the organizational system must be built." Spender then presents different types of organizational knowledge and how they interact.

The motivation for companies to become learning organizations clearly gained considerable momentum with the influential work of Senge with his "fifth discipline" work (Senge 1990 and Senge et al. 1994). This work recognizes the complexity and systemicity inherent in organizational activity and sets the theme for our discussion of "systemicity" in Chapter 5 (see in particular Kofman and Senge 1993).

Some authors describe the power of learning to transform and reinvent the organization: Coutu (2002) (quoted in Morris and Loch 2004b) interviewed by Edgar Schein said "Despite all the time, money and enthusiasm that executives pour into corporate change programs, the stark reality is that few companies ever succeed in genuinely reinventing themselves. That's because the people working at those companies more often than not fail at transformational learning—they rarely get to the point where they are eagerly challenging deeply held assumptions about a company's strategies and processes and, in response, thinking and acting in fundamentally altered ways. Rather most people just end up doing the same old things in superficially tweaked ways—practices that fall far short of the transformational learning, learning that most experts agree is the key to competing in the twenty first century."

Garvin (1993) defines and describes the "gritty details" of a learning organization. He discusses five building blocks to becoming a learning organization: *(a)* systematic problem solving, *(b)* experimentation, *(c)* learning from past experience, *(d)* learning from others, for example, benchmarking ("learning organizations . . . cultivate the art of open, attentive listening"), and *(e)* transferring knowledge, for example, reports, tours, and staff transfers. For building block *(c)*, he discusses IBM's 360 computer series, one of the most profitable ever made, which was based on a previously failed program, but he says this was by chance rather than policy and compares this with Boeing, who carried out a lessons learned after the 737 and 747 programs, and then transferred the lessons and some of the people who carried out the exercise onto the very successful 757 and 767 programs.

We are not going to summarize here all of the vast literature on organizational learning. However, key reviews of the vast literature on organizational learning can be identified. Huber (1991) gives an early and authoritative summary of the literature about organizational learning to 1991, dividing it into four aspects: knowledge acquisition, information distribution, information interpreting, organizational memory, listed in decreasing magnitude of maturity. Dodgson (1993) provides a similar bibliography of organizational learning generally, and notes the range of disciplines that contribute to the field, with organization theory plus some psychological interpretations to comprehend the process, problems, and learning. He also discusses the approaches related to economics/management/innovations, which look at the motives and source of learning, concluding also that "together, the literatures reviewed contribute to the understanding of the complexity of factors that encourage and restrict learning." Nair's (2001) literature review, charting developments in the understanding of organizational learning since the 1950's, concludes that organizational learning systems still did not have a sound theoretical base (he proposed developing a classification of organizational learning systems by their complexity as a way to learn more about them). Edmondson and Moingeon (1998) also review the literature and categorize it into four groups based on the unit of analysis and research objectives: *(a)* organizations as residues of past learning, *(b)* organizations as collections of individuals who can learn, *(c)* organizational improvement gained through intelligent activity of individual members, and *(d)* organizational improvement gained through developing individuals' mental models (note that this review is focused on the *individual* rather than the team).

Two recent authors analyze the literature with regard to the development of the field over the recent past. Bapuji and Crossan (2004) review literature on empirical organizational learning research published between 1990 and 2002, and some of their results are noted later. Easterby-Smith, Thorpe, and Lowe (2000) try to map the development of the field by reviewing the set of papers (102 in total) submitted to a particular 1999 organizational learning conference; they follow the genesis, progression, and decline of several debates in the field, some of which include:

- Debate about units of analysis: if organizational or inter-organizational learning is the sum of what individuals learn, or if there is something more (including the role of the group);

- Debate on distinguishing between changes in cognition and changes in behavior;

- Debate around single- and double-loop learning;

- Debate between organizational learning and the learning organization;

- Debate about the nature and location of organizational learning (through interpersonal interactions rather than within individuals or organizational systems);

- Debate on how to investigate organizational learning;

- Tension between the ideas of organizational learning and knowledge management;

- Shifting in focus towards a closer scrutiny of workplace activities and work practices;

- Need to reconcile learning with diversity; particularly due to globalization;

- Focus on power, politics, and trust "three fundamental dimensions of learning."

One authoritative text drawing the work together is given in the *Handbook of Organisational Learning and Knowledge* (Dierkes et al. 2001), giving 42 chapters of work ranging from insights on organizational learning from the major social science disciplines through to putting the knowledge into practice.

This body of work has contributed to a number of influential "how to" books. For example, DiBella and Nevis (1998) wrote *How Organizations Learn,* a strategic package that can be used to examine and enhance the "learning capacity" of any organization. The book describes the circumstances in which organizational learning takes place, with 10 practices or conditions which promote learning within all kinds of organizations (including experimental mind-set, climate of openness, systems perspective, etc.). It defines seven learning styles and a measurement tool for gauging an organization's performance along a continuum for each of the seven learning orientations and 10 facilitating factors. (Early versions of this work are mentioned in Nevis, DiBella, and Gould [1995]). Schwandt and Marquardt (2000) wrote *Organizational Learning: From World-Class Theories to Global Best Practices,* which presents the authors' model for organizational learning, Organizational Learning Systems Model (OLSM), which is founded on social action theory (specifically the general theory of social action posed by Talcott Parson). In addition to setting the theoretic framework for the OLSM and describing it in detail, the book also includes "action-based recommendations for organizations," recommending seven steps (said to have been gleaned from best practices in the authors' experience) towards organizational learning (using the OLSM as a frame of reference).

Two issues are clearly important in understanding organizational learning: culture and organizational structure. *Culture* plays a key role in how organizations learn and whether or not they learn. This applies both to national culture and internal corporate culture. Carmona and Grönlund (1998), for example, looked at two situations, in Sweden and Spain, whereby learning was achieved by problem-solving at the operations level. They suggest that the subsequent deterioration of learning in one of the situations presented was influenced by both the structure of the organization and national culture. High power distance and high uncertainty avoidance in Spain meant that middle managers had less responsibility and less decision-making power, so they were less able to implement changes than in Sweden. Kidd (1998) also analyzed organizational learning in some Japanese-Italian companies using Nonaka's SECI model, and found a clash of culture and context, so learning in the donor company (Japan) could not easily be translated to the receiving company (Italy). Kidd suggested that optimal learning happens in cases where there is *(a)* training by the donor company, *(b)* opportunities for peer group discussion, *(c)* empowerment at the local level (not just compliance), *(d)* appreciation of tacit knowledge held by the receiving company, and *(e)* good exchange of data. Kidd noted that elitism and rigid processes or systems were both hindrances. In terms of corporate culture, Lipshitz, Popper, and Friedman (2002) claimed that learning depended on structure, culture, psychology, policy, and context. Five cultural values that promote productive learning are: *(a)* transparency (the willingness to expose one's thoughts and actions to others in order to receive feedback), *(b)* integrity (the willingness to seek and provide info regardless of its implications), *(c)* issue-orientation (focusing on the relevance of information to the issue under consideration regardless of the social standing or rank of source or recipient), *(d)* inquiry (persisting in investigation until full understanding is achieved), and *(e)* accountability (willingness to assume responsibility for learning and implementation of lessons learned). Reger and von Wichert-Nick (1997) state that *structure and culture* of an organization are important factors in determining how effectively it can learn, which requires a culture that supports teamwork, a culture that supports experimentation and a culture that is open to risks. Wreme and Sorrenti (1997) describe cases where process consultants used systems-thinking tools with organizations to help them to learn, highlighting the importance of a safe environment for learning rather than a controlling organizational culture.

The works previously cited note the importance of *culture* and *organizational structure*. Lipshitz, Popper, and Friedman (2002) state that "For learning to become organizational, there must be roles, functions, and procedures that enable organizational members to systematically collect, analyze, store, disseminate, and use information relevant to their own and other members' performance." They use the term "organizational learning mechanisms" for "observable organizational subsystems in which organization members interact for the purpose of learning." Reger and von Wichert-Nick (1997) argue that organizational learning needs hierarchy-free communication and flow of information, a primary structure that is hierarchical and a secondary structure that is "supra-hierarchical and coordination-oriented." Carmona and Grönlund (1998) suggest that strict budgeting in an organization can constrain implementation of learning, teams need to be recognized by the rest of the organization, and the benefits of a reward system (both intrinsic [e.g., making people feel their jobs are important] and extrinsic [e.g., financial]) are important.

Bapuji and Crossan (2004) in their analysis of the empirical literature since 1990, identify facilitators to organizational learning, as well as culture and structure. They highlight strategy, environment, organizational stage, and resource position (although the contribution of the last of these is unclear). It is worth noting that Örtenblad (2002), rather than looking at structure, culture, etc., as facilitating factors to organizational learning, synthesizes the literature (including DiBella, Easterby-Smith and Araujo, Finger and Bürgin Brand, and Argyris) and sees four different meanings of the term *learning organizations*: those with organizational learning, those where people learn at work, those organizations with a learning climate, and those with a learning structure.

There are also a number of other issues that need to be considered when looking at how organizations learn. These include:

- It is important that organizations learn productively: Lipschitz, Popper, and Friedman (2002) say that "productive organizational learning is a process that is *(a)* conscious and systematic, *(b)* yields valid information and *(c)* results in actions intended to produce new perceptions, goals, and/or behavioral strategies."

- It is important to learn from a balance of both success and failures. For example, Denrell (2003) shows the bias towards success when observing management practices, because the ones that fail aren't there to be observed.

- The role of IT support is important. Venugopal and Baets (1995), for example, discuss how IT tools can support organizational learning; they describe different learning processes (learning through cases, participative strategy formation, sharing individual knowledge, and exploratory knowledge) and the IT tools which can support them (that is, in particular databases, group decision support systems, cognitive mapping, and artificial neural networks).

- The increasing use of contingent work (such as contractors), especially among high tech firms, offering reduced cost, greater flexibility, and technical expertise, can have a significant effect on a firm's ability to create and accumulate knowledge. "Contingent work can bring public knowledge into the firm, such as industry best practices; moreover, it can have a catalytic effect on the knowledge-creation process, helping to create new private [firm specific] knowledge. However, it may also act as a conduit through which private knowledge leaks into the public domain." (Matusik and Hill 1998).

2.3.4 Knowledge Management

As an organization learns, there is a need to manage proactively the knowledge within the organization. The discipline of knowledge management has been developing over a number of years. Starbuck (1992) said that "creating, applying and preserving [knowledge] intertwine and complement each other. At least over long periods, merely storing knowledge does not preserve it. For old knowledge to have meaning, people must relate it to their current problems and activities." Its importance for the development of organizations is well-recognized: for example, Coombs and Hull (1998) note the role of knowledge management in promoting innovation and describe how different knowledge management practices can influence the extent to which an organization is able to generate variety and create radically new knowledge rather than being limited by existing knowledge, shared routines, shared mental models, etc. While knowledge management is often given a fairly narrow definition, O'Dell and Jackson Grayson (1998) describe it simply as "a conscious strategy of getting the right knowledge to the right people at the right time and helping people share and put information into action in ways that strive to improve organizational performance" (cited in Levene and Gale 2000). It is now a widespread and accepted part of corporate life—for example, in the construction industry (a particularly projectized industry), Robinson, Carrillo, Anumba, and Al-Ghassani (2004) report on the state of knowledge management in 2004 in the construction industry and describe a framework for structuring and implementing a knowledge management strategy, noting the importance of linking it to business strategy and performance.

There are different types of knowledge management processes for different types of situations. Baumard's (1999) *Tacit Knowledge in Organizations,* at a basic level, quotes Nonaka's presentation giving four different ways of transferring knowledge: *(a)* tacit to tacit is socialization, *(b)* tacit to explicit is articulation, *(c)* explicit to explicit is combination, and *(d)* explicit to tacit is internalization; this book also provides a complex table of different tacit and explicit knowledge embodiments in organizations.

In a more complex level of categorization, Blackler, Crump, and McDonald (1998) divide knowledge into the following categories:

- embodied (action-oriented)

- embedded (in systemic routines)

- embrained (abstract knowledge)

- encultured and/or

- encoded (conveyed by signs and symbols).

These categories use a number of types of knowledge processes, such as:

* provisional and reflexive (actively and creatively constructed rather than eternal verities)

* mediated by linguistic and technological infrastructure (people operate within interpretive or discourse communities)

* situated and pragmatic

* contested and political

* emotional as well as rational.

Although a full treatment of the huge literature on knowledge management in general is outside of the scope of this book, a few relevant summaries of the field will be referenced. von Krogh, Roos, and Kleine (1998) give an overview of the state of the art in 1998. In terms of actual practice, Ruggles (1998) describes some knowledge management activities, based on a study of over 400 organizations and which include barriers to successful implementation. Prichard, Hull, Chumer, and Willmott (2000) give a compilation of articles that provide critical perspectives on work and organization. Specifically, broad perspectives on the developmental aspects of knowledge management, particularly exploring (*inter al*) the impact of knowledge management on the working life of professionals, the effect of knowledge management upon the internal mechanisms within organizations, issues relating to decision-making, and the extraction of wealth from knowledge. And of particular note, Scarbrough, Swan, and Preston (1999) give a full review of literature on knowledge management and learning organizations from 1993 through 1998. They note that literature regarding learning organizations has been declining in the latter years while that on knowledge management was increasing, largely in the IS/IT literature, much of it in practitioner-oriented journals: "The dominant discourse of KM [Knowledge Management] (to capture, codify, use and exploit the knowledge and experience of employees by developing better tools and methods and by developing a willingness and ability to use those methods) is fundamentally different to that of the LOs [Learning Organizations] (to harness the learning capability of the firm and individuals within it through people development, empowerment, leadership and culture change)."

A number of authors have warned against the frequency with which knowledge management work restricts its attention to knowledge that can be codified. Johnson, Lorenz, and Lundvall (2002) make the common distinction between know-what, know-why, know-how, and know-who knowledge and note that learning isn't simply about codifying knowledge. When deciding whether to codify knowledge, one needs to take into account both the amount that will be lost in the transformation process and whether codification is an improvement or not (although they recognize that codification can stimulate learning when used to refine models and create shared vocabulary and to support the process of reflection, explication, and documentation of practices). Connell, Klein, and Powell (2003) cover the literature on knowledge management and point to shortcomings with both the personalization view of knowledge management (knowledge is considered inseparable from the person or group that holds it) and the codification view (knowledge is seen as a commodity which can be isolated and codified); they make the point that one needs to consider knowledge as a property of the system, and knowledge needs to be embedded within the context.

The concentration on codification is perhaps due to the frequent view of knowledge management (KM) as part of IT. Scarbrough, Swan, and Preston (1999) quote Cole-Gomolski (1997), who states "the idea behind knowledge management is to stockpile workers' knowledge and make it accessible to others via a searchable application" to illustrate the view that KM consists simply of making a database. Venugopal and Baets (1995) do take a wide view of how IT tools can support organizational learning (as was seen in 1995). They describe different learning processes (for example, cases, participative strategy formation, sharing individual knowledge, and exploratory knowledge) and the IT tools that can support them (database, group decision support system, cognitive mapping, and artificial neural networks). McDermott (1999) has already been quoted previously as warning that IT cannot deliver knowledge. In more detail, Scarbrough, Swan, and Preston (1999) talk about the problem of knowledge management being only interested in IT solutions: "This obsession with tools and techniques falls foul of at least four basic problems. First, it assumes that all knowledge is codifiable, which clearly it is not . . . Secondly, it overemphasizes the utility new information technologies have for delivering organization performance improvements . . . Third, it assumes that, even if perfect systems existed, people are willing to make them work, i.e. to contribute their knowledge to the systems, to share their knowledge and to use the knowledge from the systems, which clearly they are not, or at least not readily. Fourth, the codification and objectification of all tacit knowledge into formal systems . . . generates its own psychopathy – i.e. the fluid, organic, informal and intuitive practices that are essential in allowing the flexible firm to cope with uncertainty will rigidify."

Stein and Zwass (1995) indicate that while an organizational memory system can both support and impede higher level learning, an over reliance on it can lessen the degree to which people will question underlying assumptions and procedures and engage in exploratory learning.

2.4 **The Current Situation**

2.4.1 **Standards and Maturity Models**

Which standards are used for drawing lessons from projects? This is such a key element of project management that one might expect that there should be clearly defined guidelines and ways of measuring an organization's effectiveness at learning project lessons.

Morris, Patel, and Wearne (2000) in their research used to revise the British project management "Body of Knowledge" (BoK) looked into what should actually be included in a BoK, and 80% of project practitioners agreed that "post-project evaluation review" should be included. In the expanded version of the British BoK, the Pathways book, Wateridge authors a chapter on project-implementation reviews (which considers "the reasons behind the variances between the plan and actual spend and effort" and "what would have been done differently with the benefit of hindsight"), project health-checks (which look at the stakeholders' view of the direction of the project and whether the project as a whole is moving in the direction to succeed), and project audits (particularly looking at fraud), although this chapter only gives general guidance (Wateridge 2002).

The Project Management Institute's *A Guide to the Project Management Body of Knowledge (PMBOK® Guide* – Third Edition), an ANSI standard and the basis of PMI's professional qualification, gives the simple statement that "The causes of variances, the reasoning behind the corrective action chosen, and other types of lessons learned should be documented so that they become part of the historical database . . ." (Section 8.3.3.8). Strang (2003) notes the fact that lessons learned are included as inputs or outputs to almost all of the nine knowledge areas of the *PMBOK® Guide*, and in all five process groups (and details many of the relevant subsections). Strang looks at theory about organizational learning in projects and looks at practice but concludes that the theory is rarely applied in practice and discusses the difficulties. Lessons learned do come into the Project Management Institute's OPM3 Organizational Project Management Maturity Model (Project Management Institute 2004), but with little emphasis or much guidance beyond the *PMBOK® Guide*.

PRINCE2 (Office of Government Commerce 2002) also has a process for recording lessons learned and reporting on them. Lessons are captured in the lessons learned log; at the end of the project these are collated into a lessons learned report.

It is not just the project management BoKs that recognize this need: Turner et al. (2000) describe the use of procedures to represent captured knowledge and experience and stress the vital role of project reviews and say that "End of project reviews play a vital part in capturing experience within organizations. PRINCE2 and ISO 10006 suggest a review be conducted at the end of every project, and company standard procedures updated to reflect this."

So the standards generally require project reviews to be carried out, although with little guidance as to how this should operate. But is "learning lessons" featured in the more sophisticated "maturity models" that seek to define how mature an organization is in project management? Cooke-Davies and Arzymanow (2002) describe a study looking at how practices in project management differ between industries, carried out for a community of practice of project managers in the pharmaceutical industry; they identified different levels of maturity in different industries but do not discuss differences in the way organizations learn. Nor did recent work on Organizational Project Management Maturity (e.g., Kalantjakos 2001); nor really the risk management maturity model standard (Risk Management Research and Development Program Collaboration 2002), in which there is no significant discussion of post-project analysis and no closing the learning loop ("Level 3" has some data collection, and "Level 4" has a direct mention of "learning by experience"). But recent maturity standards work reported in Schlichter (2001) required the following:

- A process to capture and disseminate lessons learned

- "Lessons learned" stored in an accessible location

- Evidence of capture/dissemination and the reuse of information in subsequent projects.

Further, he looked for learning from projects that is translated into the corporate approach, and learning that takes place in all of its dimensions (i.e., individual, team, organizational).

Another work building further on this is from von Zedtwitz (2002), who gives a capability model only for post-project reviews. Using the standard five-stage capability model, he defines stages:

- *Initial:* ad-hoc methods, reaction-driven reviews

- *Repeatable:* with sound review practices

- *Defined:* a standardized process with sound and consistent review criteria, "usually" with a small unit responsible for training

- *Managed:* review goals with "quantified and measurable" quality criteria

- *Optimized:* post-project reviews established organization-wide with proactive review of processes.

2.4.2 Prevalence

Given that the standards do require project reviews to be carried out, the literature is somewhat divided regarding its prevalence in practice.

Some papers state as an accepted fact that learning is rare. Gulliver (1987) says "in talking with business people from large British and multi-national corporations, I have found that few companies examine their completed projects in any depth." Harris agrees, saying that "learning from past mistakes, or even building upon past successes, continues to be the exception rather than the rule." Disterer (2002) says that "Only a few firms manage systematically to identify and transfer valuable knowledge from projects to following projects." Carrillo et al. (2004) state that in construction management—a particularly relevant field as it is project-based—"... teams frequently disband upon project completion without conducting post-project reviews and disseminating the lessons learned." Keegan and Turner's (2001) research suggested that "learning was unsatisfactory."

Some papers on the other hand state as accepted fact that generally lessons learned activities and learning from projects generally occur in practice. Newell (2004) describes post-mortems as "ubiquitous." Scarbrough, Swan, and Preston (1999) comment that "as firms increasingly become more innovative and project-based, many are recognizing the need to capture the learning from individual projects, and make it available throughout the organization. Consultancies, professional service firms, aerospace companies, etc., are in the vanguard of developing systems to codify and communicate such knowledge."

More useful, of course, is actual statistics on the prevalence of project learning activity (this current PMI project will of course provide some large-sample statistics in a later document). None of the results give definitive or conclusive conclusions. Many describe post-project review as fairly common:

- Besner and Hobbs (2004) describe a survey of the usage of project management (PM) tools and techniques across different contexts and project types, in which "Lessons learned/post-mortem" is one of the most frequently used on all project types; however, the use of "database of lessons learned" differed significantly between low and high PM maturity organizations.

- Kotnour's (2000) influential paper was based on a survey of 43 project managers who were attending a PMI chapter meeting (so could be expected to be interested generally in project management learning)—of these, 31 said they completed lessons while 12 said they did not.

- Carrillo et al. (2004) (with 53 responses in the construction field) found that 26% of companies did not have (or plan to have) a knowledge management strategy (although only 9.5% in the case of companies with more than 1,500 employees)

- Fong (2005) describes a survey of knowledge management among quantity surveyors in Hong Kong and the UK: in a table of "practices used," "lessons learned from previous projects" came in as the third most common practice in the UK and fifth in Hong Kong (although it wasn't clear whether this referred to formalized procedures or not); however, this was clearly not seen as sufficient in terms of what they wanted their companies to develop, 43% wanted them to develop knowledge-sharing skills, 39% wanted them to develop knowledge-capturing skills, and 18% knowledge-creating skills.

Others, on the other hand, found post-project reviews to be less frequent:

- An early piece of research here is described in Neale and Holmes (1990), who carried out a survey of finance directors from companies (with 410 replies) about their post-auditing procedures for capital projects (so the emphasis is on improving decisions about whether to invest in a project, e.g., better proposals, better evaluation, better financial control): 48% used post-auditing techniques, with a bias towards the largest companies (large being a relative term as all the companies were taken from the Times 1000) and manufacturing companies.

- An influential paper by von Zedtwitz (2002) describes a survey of R&D projects with 63 responses, in which "80% of all R&D projects are not reviewed at all after completion, and most of the remaining 20% were reviewed without established review guidelines."

- Menke (1997) describes a study of 79 R&D companies which gives ten best practices for R&D decisions and which confer R&D competitive advantage. 'Learning from post-project audits' is seen as one of the ten practices which confer R&D advantage but comes in bottom place in looking at how often they occur—in only 24% of companies.

- Lilly and Porter's study (2003) of new product development companies found that "Improvement reviews are a low priority ... most interviewed firms conduct reviews only on selected projects, for example major or unique projects."

Azzone and Maccarrone (2001) in a survey of Italian firms (with 34 responses) give more detailed results. Their results seem to indicate that post-audit is more prevalent in larger firms, and that post-auditing practices differ depending on the reasons for doing it.

Finally, Themistocleous and Wearne (2000), looking at the project management literature, noted that: "[post-] project evaluation review (the only place for "learning") was mentioned in only 1% (4/339) of the papers published in *International Journal of Project Management* and 1% (3/210) of the papers in *Project Management Journal*."

2.5 Creating Knowledge

2.5.1 Practices

Given that it is accepted that lessons learned activities *should* be carried out—how should it actually be done? This section will look at practices for collecting lessons and creating knowledge in the first place— Section 2.6 will look at practices for disseminating knowledge once created.

Learning starts with the individual. Practices require individuals firstly to retain information, then to reflect upon and learn from it. The most straightforward suggestion is keeping some sort of journal or diary to retain information. Loo (2002) reports on the use of "learning diaries," concluding that they can be useful, but the user has to think about how to do it and believe in their value. Rigano and Edwards (1998) describe a case study on journal keeping and reflection as tools for individual learning, based on interviews and analysis of the journal of an engineer employed in a large refinery over 15 months. (Kransdorff [1996]) feels that a more appropriate method is the use of oral logs, using an independent researcher.) But it is this element of reflection that is key: the journal is useful if it is reflected upon, and Rigano and Edwards go on to outline the theoretic background to "reflection" and quote various authors on the topic. Indeed, as alluded to in Section 2.3, there is a whole body of work based on the idea of reflective practitioners, much based on the work of Schön (1991). Smith (2001), who claims that "most of the time we have experiences from which we never learn," describes a framework and tools for reflective learning in an organization.

As we'll discuss in Section 2.5.2, much value can be gained from recording stories rather than simple "lessons." NASA is a prime example: "NASA strives to promote communication and wisdom transfer through knowledge management. Typical of most project managers, our staff doesn't want to hang around at a project's completion to write memoirs; team members want to move on to the next big, exciting project. However, we must stress the importance of taking time for lessons learned. We must continue to ascertain how NASA can become better by reflection and application of our experiences. . . . For this purpose, NASA has established an in-depth knowledge-sharing program. APPL [the Academy of Program and Project Leadership] sponsors short forums allowing project managers to share their lessons through stories, as in our internal magazine ASK (http://www.appl. nasa.gov/)" (Hoffman 2003). Stories can be valuable in comparing different projects; for example, Newcombe (2000) uses vignettes to compare two projects (in tandem with looking at the overall projects). Another mechanism sometimes used is the "micro article" (Schindler and Eppler [2003] quoting the original source of Helmut Wilke), which is a half-page documentation of experiences and their context.

But as we look at organizational practices, we need to move from the individual to group practices (Barker and Neailey 1999).

One common procedure is to have a review group looking at the project after its conclusion. British Petroleum's Post Project Appraisal (PPA) Unit, described in Gulliver's (1987) influential article, assessed about six projects each year, with a team of two or three people taking about six months to complete each review. In Azzone and Maccarrone's (2001) survey, most firms used a team of three members to do the review; 50% of the review teams were external to the project (preferred by those performing a review for learning purposes) and 41% "hybrid" (internal and external members; preferred by those performing the review for control purposes). The U.S. Army also deploys teams to collect lessons and create archives which can be accessed by the whole organization (Crosman 2002). The Texas State Agencies' guidelines (Texas Department of Information Resources 2000) state as a given that "an objective facilitator runs the process"; Schindler and Eppler (2003) say that an external, neutral moderator is a key success factor for the process; Kransdorff (1996) also recommends that there should be at least an independent researcher involved, and Abramovici (1999) recommends an independent facilitator.

A well-regarded procedure for developing and recording the progress of a project is the "Learning History," a written document chronologically describing the main events of a project with a storytelling type of approach, in a particular structure including both direct quotations from the participants and commentary from the analysts preparing the history. The approach was developed by Roth and Kleiner (1998) and is quoted in various reviews and structures (e.g., Levene and Gale 2000 and Schindler and Eppler 2003).

A second common practice is to hold a group meeting to look at the project as a whole and draw lessons. In Ericsson's methods, described in Brander-Löf, Hilger, and André et al. (2000), regular meetings were held involving all project members, since "People will, while concentrating on their work tasks, recognize simpler cause-effect relationships, but more complex patterns that might span across the whole organization are more likely to be uncovered only by a systematic learning effort" (referring to Wheelwright and Clark 1992). Abramovici (1999) uses open and facilitated brain-storming sessions. Collier, DeMarco, and Fearey's (1996) defined process for post-mortems of IT projects included some stages of collecting data and debriefing, but then followed by a "project history day," involving six to eight people and a facilitator, with the aim of identifying root causes. Bullard (2005) even suggests including the customer (or at least the customer's viewpoint) into account in the lessons learned activity. (Deane, Clark, and Young [1997] do not suggest including the customer, but do suggest reviewing the project by comparing the output with the customer requirements). Schindler and Eppler (2003) stress that this meeting should be interactive. (For further discussion about "rules" for post-project meeting discussions, see Kerth's [2000] descriptions of his "retrospectives" with IS teams.) Busby's (1999b) study covered simply post-project review meetings.

It will be seen that a key reason for including a larger group is to help to explore root causes or systemic effects. This will be explored further in Section 2.5.3, but it is worth noting here one particular technique that arises in a number of these discussions: the use of mapping or similar structuring methods to explore or explicate systemicity. In the Ericsson methods (Brander-Löf, Hilger, and André 2000), a post-it session and mapping were used in the project review meeting. Venugopal and Baets' (1995) discussion of intelligent support systems for organizational learning describe different "IT tools" including cognitive mapping. Williams et al. (2005) describe a major case study showing why learning lessons is difficult, and why (and how) mapping was used to learn lessons (and how some lessons learned were used to feed back into the formal Project Risk Management process). Williams (2004) describes a case study of using mapping in a manufacturing company to learn lessons post-mortem. Franco, Cushman, and Rosenhead (2004) widen this out to describe various problem structuring methods, specifically strategic choice, for inter-organizational post-project reviews.

Another reason for such meetings or similar structures is the underlying complexity both in projects and thus in the resulting project history. Boddy and Paton (2004) point out that people involved in a project often express diametrically opposite accounts of events, thus the analyst needs to take account of competing narratives which arise from project complexity; they suggest firstly carrying out stakeholder analysis and secondly creating structures to enable alternative views to be articulated. This will be explored further as we look at narratives and storytelling in Section 2.5.2.

However, such procedures should not be only at the end of a project but during a project also. This can be particularly important for a long project: "A project may last for several years. Valuable learning experiences take place at the beginning of the project, but are not captured until the post-project review at the end" (Turner, Keegan, and Crawford 2000). Kotnour (2000) points out that lessons learned activities can be conducted throughout a project life cycle, not just at the end; Bullard (2005) emphasizes the need for regular "milestone reviews" prior to a final post-mortem or lessons learned, to capture the information while it is still fresh; Schindler and Eppler (2003) say that this is a key success factor for the process; Lilly and Porter (2003) say that reviews should be conducted at various stages of the project, not just at the end, since reviews conducted at different stages have different foci. In Ericsson's methods, described in Brander-Löf, Hilger, and André (2000), review meetings were held every three months. In SmithKline Beecham, there is "a regular structured ongoing project review process" (Gibson and Pfautz 1999) based on key milestones. Englund and Graham (1999) talk about how Hewlett-Packard carried out lessons learned to resolve a set of interrelated issues, setting up study groups to explore possible solutions, holding regular meetings to review progress and make changes, supported by senior managers.

Different types of projects and different objectives need different techniques for analysis and drawing out lessons. The Texas State Agencies' guidelines (Texas Department of Information Resources 2000) describe tailoring the activities undertaken, the roles of the various participants, and the deliverables depending on whether there is a low, medium, or high "QA focus." It is interesting to note that one third of the sample in Crawford, Hobbs, and Turner's (2004) survey quoted "lessons learned" as one of the reasons they used a project-categorization system. Schindler and Eppler (2003) give a simple table showing four sets of approaches and their different aspects (covering time carried out, by whom, participants, purpose, benefits, interaction mode, and codification), which illustrates the aspects that need to be considered when choosing a method. Kotnour (2000) describes the results of his survey, showing the frequencies with which practices were found to fall into categories for: *(a)* how a project knows what to produce a lesson learned about, *(b)* what is included in lesson learned, *(c)* tasks about which the lesson learned is produced, and *(d)* when a lesson learned is produced. Of course many circumstances will require a mixture of methods. Schoeniger (2005), for example, looks (also) at Hewlett-Packard methods for knowledge capture, with knowledge management integrated into processes, lessons learned captured through post-project reviews, intranet resources, communities-of-practice forums, best practices, etc.

The most complete collections of techniques are given in the landscapes given by Brady et al. (2002) and Prencipe and Tell (2001) (both based on the work of Zollo and Winter 2002). These papers give learning mechanisms in a matrix of learning processes (divided into experience accumulation, knowledge articulation, and knowledge codification) against organizational level (individual, group, and organizational). This table leads to three "ideal types" of approaches: the *L*-shaped "socially driven approach" (in firms that rely significantly on people-embedded knowledge); the *T*-shaped "broadly socio-technical" approach, and the "staircase" landscape (including firms "involved in the advanced development of ICT-based tools to support inter-project learning). These tables not only give a useful brief compendium of methods, they also provide helpful categorizations that indicate the appropriate points of use and the techniques more appropriate for a particular organization.

2.5.2 Narratives

As the practices previously mentioned move into areas such as learning histories (Roth and Kleiner 1998), the discussion transitions from statements of facts and lessons learned to the ideas of stories and narratives. Increasingly, in recent years, the use of stories appears to be more important than deriving lessons from projects. Polkinghorne (1988) says that narratives are a key way in which we get to know the "primary form by which human experience is made meaningful." Boje (1991) describes storytelling as "the institutional memory system of the organization."

There is an abundance of literature about storytelling and narratives in organizations (Boyce [1996] gives a good bibliography). Perhaps the best-known text is Gabriel's (2000) book, *Storytelling in Organisations: Facts, Fictions and Fantasies*. He looks at how stories are used in organizations, and how important narratives are in providing the memory of the organization. He describes how stories invite us to engage with the meaning as stories describe the experience of the teller. He distinguishes between reports (facts-as-description) and stories (facts-as-experience), but talks about both. (Note that because a search for lessons needs to look for the reasoning behind management behavior, stories must be a key factor.) "Story work involves the transformation of everyday experience into meaningful stories. In doing so, the storytellers neither accept nor reject 'reality.' Instead, they seek to mold it, shape it, and infuse it with meaning, each in a distinct and individual way through the use of poetic tropes." Gabriel describes eight of these "poetic tropes." Five appear to be important for our purposes in providing analysis of project events: attribution of motive, attribution of causal connection, attribution of responsibility (blame/credit), attribution of emotion, and attribution of agency. The other three are attribution of unity (i.e., not differentiating within a class of people "they"), attribution of fixed qualities (especially in opposition, e.g., "once a liar always a liar"), and attribution of providential significance. Gabriel does not view narratives as the entire answer to how to learn lessons. He warns against the danger of regarding everything as narrative and losing sight of the importance of actual events and notes in particular that "researchers who want to use stories as a research instrument must be prepared to sacrifice at least temporarily some of the core values of their craft . . . they must rid themselves of the assumption that quality data must be objective, reliable, accurate etc . . . at the same time researchers must not lose sight of the relation between stories and facts: facts are not dissolved by stories but recreated through them." These poetic tropes are vital in understanding how projects turn out the way they do, particularly in the light of the systemic aspects that will be discussed in the next section. (Gabriel also gives a full bibliography on organizational narratives and provides a taxonomy.)

As well as the promotion of various attribution modes, why are narratives important? The key reason is that projects are by their nature complex, and the reasons underlying project outcomes often are complex (which will be explored further in Section 2.5.3). Tsoukas and Hatch (2001) give a major paper on complexity and the subsequent need for narratives. They describe how complexity is not only a feature of the system but always of the way we organize our thinking about those systems that they term second-order complexity; they cite Bruner differentiating between logico-scientific and narrative thinking, and describe how, because of the nature of complexity, there are problems with the former and the latter is more suitable. They also cite White, who says that narrative recreates the world; it includes causality, motive, and temporality. Connell, Klein, and Meyer et al. (2004) show how stories carry with them the complex organizational context which is important for knowledge management. Linehan and Kavanagh (2004) observe that the dominant ontology in project management is a "being" ontology, over-emphasizing reification and representation (ironically as project management was set up to replace production management), rather than "becoming" ontology, which emphasizes sense-making and questions boundaries. "Projects are complex, ambiguous, confusing phenomena wherein the idea of a single, clear goal is at odds with the reality," and they say that narratives expose subtle project dynamics and transient actions, which often are difficult to pin down. Nocker (2004) uses the ideas of Lefebvre on the idea of social space (which is produced, not a "thing in itself"), and tells the story of an IT project in which narratives were the only way to make sense of the project, saying "narratives offer a view of the multiple nature, and I hope a more comprehensive understanding of the 'project as emergent space.'"

Another reason why narratives are useful is because actual practice often differs from company procedures or norms. Brown and Duguid (1991) state that "the ways people actually work usually differ fundamentally from the ways organizations formally describe that work (that is, there is noncanonical as well as canonical practice), and learning happens not just by transmitting explicit knowledge but also by acquiring tacit knowledge within a communal context." In practice, they say, people form informal communities of practice which are "often noncanonical and not recognized by the organization. They are more fluid and interpenetrative than bounded, often crossing the restrictive boundaries of the organization to incorporate people from outside . . . And significantly, communities are emergent. That is to say their shape and membership emerges in the process of activity, as opposed to being created to carry out a task." Learning and innovation happen within these communities and need to be recognized and supported. Their thesis is illustrated by Orr's account (1990) of situated learning by storytelling (photocopier repair workers); the documentation (and training) was inadequate for fixing machines, so workers used storytelling of previous experiences to develop causal maps of the machines; this mode of learning was neither recognized nor supported by the organization. Exactly the same use of project stories is discussed by Koskinen (2005), saying that "since the actual work practice often differs from the canonical practice described in manuals and directive documents, the community of practice plays an important role for socialising and sharing experiences of workarounds and trouble shooting," differentiating between project implementation stories (solving particular problems within individual projects) and project company stories (shared by everyone in the project-based company). The latter are useful at project start-up meetings, but "knowledge encoded in project company stories may be lost when existing patterns of interaction are repeatedly broken up or not allowed to form as is often the case for project companies. Firms that fail to reinforce storytelling may experience a loss of knowledge as relationships atrophy."

Story transmission, and sometimes even story development, is a social process. "Story work is not always a purely personal process. Some stories are virtually multi-authored, being co-narrated simultaneously . . . others emerge accidentally during conversations out of small narrative fragments" Gabriel (2000). Abma (2003) looks into the meaning and value of storytelling workshops within the context of organizational learning using a study of the practice of palliative care in a Dutch health care authority, and notes that "a storytelling workshop is a social event and this resonates with the idea of a social infrastructure or architecture, platform or network to stimulate the exchange of experiences and to "anchor" learning processes in the working community"; storytelling is described as both a "dialogical," "divergent," "emergent," and "collaborative" process. This enables the multiple meanings of stories to be explored; Boje's (1995) well-known deconstruction of stories of one organization (Walt Disney) for example stresses parallel storytelling (plurivocality), and he explores the "polyserious" or multiple meanings of the stories. One particular benefit of the social aspect of storytelling is that it enables the emotional aspect of events to be retained; MacMaster (2000), for example, points out the limitations of relying on objective project documentation alone for learning and the benefits of combining it with subjective perceptions such as through storytelling; Gabriel (2000) refers to analytical work that misses the emotional quality of stories. For example, Wilkins (1984) refers to a map (in this case using stories as a map for a new recruit to the organization), while Gabriel talks about painting a landscape.

2.5.3 Systemicity

Projects are complex entities and learning from complex systems needs a more sophisticated approach than simply writing down lessons learned. Eden, Ackermann, and Williams (2005) and Eden et al. (2000) following Williams et al. (1995) and Williams, Ackermann, and Tait (1995) give a good explanation of complexity in projects, showing how chains of causality build up to complex systems of relationships, often causing combinations that appear greater than the sum of their parts. In particular, they describe situations where positive feedback builds up and explain the need for new paradigms for complex projects (Williams 1999). The two items here then are firstly recognizing or identifying causality: "Causality, then, is part of the design that reason imposes on experience to make it understandable," (Von Glasersfeld 1995) and secondly and particularly systemicity: McKenna (1999), for example, gives a general paper on complexity faced by managers and the need to create a mechanism to identify, analyze, and learn. (He used simple maps to show intra-organized relationships.) Similarly, Senge (1990), talking two years after *The Fifth Discipline*, highlights the need for systemic thinking so that the proper lessons can be learned, to move to the "learning organization" (Kofman and Senge 1993).

What does this mean then about how managers learn about complex systems (in general)? Morecroft (2004) claims that "learning" about complex systems means developing mental models of the systems, which he says is aided through the use of a formal model (such as, in his case, system dynamics). Similarly, Sterman (2000) claims that managers have a propensity to misperceive the implications of longer-term feedbacks, which he attributes to a fundamental deficiency in thinking that he calls "flawed mental maps," at the heart of Simon's theory of bounded rationality (referenced in Simon 1991) (again proposing system dynamics as a method to enhance learning in complex systems). Kim (1993) similarly shows the links between individual and organizational learning by means of "shared mental models" and discusses the best sort of models for dynamic complexity, which is where learning is important and difficult. Wreme and Sorrenti (1997) describe cases where process consultants used systems thinking tools with organizations to help them to learn, surfacing mental models using tools such as Senge's *5 whys*, graphical representations, and causal loop diagrams.

Zollo and Winter (2002) claim that the relative effectiveness of their three types of learning behaviors (noted in Section 2.3.2) depends on the nature of the task. In particular, knowledge codification activities (and to a lesser extent articulation) are more effective than tacit accumulation for tasks that are *(a)* less frequent, *(b)* less homogeneous, and, of particular interest here, *(c)* with greater causal ambiguity. Causal ambiguity is contrary to current practice, since organizations are more likely to codify knowledge for routine operations, but say codification should be about *know why* as well as *know how* and aim to expose causal links.

Apart from the one very good technique already looked at—the use of "narratives"—how does this relate to the manner in which we learn lessons from projects, where these problems are particularly relevant (Williams, Ackermann, and Colin 2003)? The points previously mentioned about management systems in general are echoed in the studies of project reviews, with a number of authors expressing concern about the need for, and difficulty of, looking at underlying systemicity. Busby's (1999a) study of post-project review meetings found the diagnosis shallow because of a preference for causal rather than diagnostic reasoning (as noted previously, diagnostic learning is harder and there are social implications but it leads to deeper diagnosis) and not enough "why." von Zedtwitz (2002) outlined four "barriers to success" (or rather, categories of barriers) in his study of organizational learning through post-project reviews in R&D, one of which was epistemological, including systemicity. Liu and Walker (1998) conclude that there are three main problems with using post-project evaluation to identify critical success factors in a (construction) project, one of which is that identifying causality is difficult, so the causal relationships identified might be wrong. Brander-Löf, Hilger, and André (2000), in outlining a procedure for lessons learned developed at Ericsson, said that "people will, while concentrating on their work tasks, recognize simpler cause-effect relationships, but more complex patterns that might span across the whole organization are more likely to be uncovered only by a systematic learning effort."

The penultimate "project history day" stage of Collier, DeMarco, and Fearey's (1996) defined process for post-mortem review of IS projects has the aim of identifying root causes. Pitagorsky (2000) says that in learning lessons from projects, process thinking and review are essential, for example, to identify cause-and-effect chains. Busby's (1999a) study looking at the effectiveness of post-mortems highlighted issues with lack of diagnostic reasoning: "didn't get to the bottom of it, it only identified the fact that problems are there." Cooper, Lyneis, and Bryant (2002) say that the difficulty in determining the true causes of project performance inhibits learning. Lynn, Reilly, and Akgun (2000) note the need to take a systemic view in looking at lessons (in NPD projects): "As Solomon (1994) states, 'Traditional way of handling complexity prevents us from seeing the larger picture . . . People have a tendency to break problems down into smaller pieces so that they are more manageable. However, the difficulty with this reductionism type of thinking is that it assumes that the sum of the parts equals the whole.' Looking at one, two, or even a handful of factors to solve a complex problem is focusing only on the tip of the iceberg. Team members need to consider the interaction of interrelated factors in the NPD process. They need to think more broadly, more holistically, and consider the multidimensional nature of the team learning system."

Some methods for looking at systemicity have already been explored in the previous two sections. Franco, Cushman, and Rosenhead (2004) describe the use of problem-structuring methods, specifically strategic choice, for inter-organizational post-project reviews in the construction industry. Perhaps the most prominent method of displaying and analyzing systemicity is the use of mapping. Williams (2004) describes a case study using mapping to uncover systemicity and learn lessons in a project post-mortem. Williams, Ackermann, and Eden (2003) describe a more structured approach to develop a full and detailed understanding of the systemic causes and effects in a project post-mortem for a post-project litigation situation. A natural development of the use of causal mapping is to develop quantitative system dynamics simulation models of a project: Graham (2000) describes at a simple level the work of PA in developing such models and drawing post-project lessons (following early work such as Cooper [1994]); Lyneis et al. (2001) and Cooper, Lyneis, and Bryant (2002) give deeper and more detailed analyses of PA's modeling. Similar work has been done by the Eden/Williams/Ackermann/Howick school, with mapping and system dynamics modeling combined in a methodological framework as described in Ackermann, Eden, and Williams (1997) and Williams et al. (2005); the first of these two references emphasizes the need to look at projects with mixed methods, to gain a full understanding. Boddy and Paton (2004) similarly point out that project participants often express diametrically opposite accounts of events; and methods to analyze projects need to take into account the competing narratives which arise from project complexity. In a more conventional mode, Fortune and Peters (1995) claim that people do not learn from mistakes and therefore present a highly developed and well-tested systems methodology to analyze, understand, and predict failures called the systems failures method (SFM), based on systems thinking. It is worth noting that Mitev (1998, p. 53) claims that their "quest to explain all . . . through the 'disciplined approach of systems engineering' epitomizes a belief in universal and scientific solutions" results in the lessons learned which are too broad, superficial, and contradictory to be universal.

2.5.4 Facilitating Factors and Hindrances

The literature gives various advice on what inhibits the collection of lessons learned and the creation of knowledge, or conversely what facilitates such collection. Much of this advice has been covered in Sections 2.5.1 to 2.5.3 previously, but this section is intended to draw the remaining advice together.

A key inhibitor is clearly the lack of time available to undertake such exercises. In Carillo and others' (2004) survey, 68% stated "not enough time" as a main barrier to learning. Keegan and Turner (2001) cite inadequate time and too many other pressures as inhibitors (also too much focus on retention/exploitation and not enough on exploration). Pan and Flynn (2003) quote lack of time as a reason for a failed lessons learned exercise. Styhre, Josephson, and Knauseder (2004) call for more slack to allow for discussions and training, and cite practical difficulties of arranging a meeting after the project team has dispersed as a significant problem. Schindler and Eppler (2003) also point to the difficulty in coordinating debriefings when people are engaged in new projects, and also point out that there is particular time pressure towards the project's end. Zollo and Winter (2002) (using Tyre and Orlikowski) state that "Opportunity cost considerations [deriving from the sacrifice of time dedicated to working on active projects] have the somewhat paradoxical effect of tending to suppress learning when it is most valuable and needed: The higher the activity levels in the execution of a certain task, the higher the opportunity costs for the learning investments dedicated to that specific task, and therefore the lower the likelihood that the hyperactive team will afford the time to debrief, despite the obvious advantages from the potential identification of process improvements."

Clearly related to the issue of time are the issues of which incentives there are for team members to contribute to organizational learning and which resources are available to carry out the exercises. Neale and Holmes (1990) indicate that an important deterrent to introducing post auditing is that it is costly to do. In Carrillo and others' (2004) survey, 62% quoted "not enough money" and 49% stated "employee resistance" as main barriers. Bresnen et al. (2002) cite incentives and resources as key factors enabling organizational learning; "implementing reward systems that encourage people to engage in thoughtful dialogue" is one of Kotnour and Hjelm's (2002) five management actions to encourage learning; Keegan and Turner (2001) claim that inadequate resources is a cause of unsatisfactory learning. Pitagorsky (2000) said that one common barrier is the "lack of awareness of the connection between process review, lessons learned, and process improvement" so that workers are unwilling to allocate time. More generally, Nonaka (1991) said that the key reasons for tapping tacit knowledge are "personnel commitment, the employees' sense of identity with the enterprise, and its mission" (quoted by Scarbrough, Swan, and Preston 1999). The issue of available resources depends on senior management support. Crosman (2002), for example, talking about lessons learned in the U.S. Army says that establishing a lessons learned process needs management support (Neale and Letza [1996] make this point also; Pan and Flynn [2003] likewise call for the commitment of senior management). (On incentives, Winch [1998] notes the increase in sub-contract/self-employed workers in the British construction industry and suggests that this takes away the incentive to provide organizational learning.)

A key set of facilitating or inhibiting factors relate to the social and behavioral processes involved in capturing knowledge (Bresnen et al. 2003). In Carrillo and others' (2004) survey, 76% quoted organizational culture as a barrier. Kotnour and Hjelm's (2002) other four management actions to encourage learning (following the one mentioned in the previous paragraph) are part of the organizational culture: making learning an organizational goal, reinforcing the learning mind-set of leaders, encouraging experimentation, and building a community of learners (this last activity will be included in the discussion of communities of practice later). In particular, a blame culture will inhibit learning (Pitagorsky [2000], Neale and Holmes [1990], and Busby [1999b])—Busby also interestingly notes that the norm of constructive criticism inhibits criticism with no immediate solutions. Styhre et al. (2004) say that when a meeting does happen it's easier just to praise one another and not address the problems. Glanville (2003) gave an authoritative presentation claiming that factors which can limit the effectiveness of project status reviews include fear of failure, ambition, unwillingness to speak about difficult issues, threat that the project might be stopped or curtailed, and a desire to justify the past rather than manage the future. Two of Schindler and Eppler's (2003) reasons for failing to learn lessons are "insufficient willingness for learning from mistakes of the persons involved," and "missing communication of the experience . . . due to 'wrong modesty' . . . or the fear of negative sanctions." Morris and Loch (2004a) point to "culture and strategic intent" as "very evident influences" in their empirical work. Pan and Flynn (2003) discuss a case study of a failed project in a Japanese organization, where there was a strong, collective culture that inhibited people from criticizing others and jeopardizing relationships; people were embarrassed by failure and saw it as a threat to their job security. "Maintaining social relationships typically matters more to most people than accurate diagnoses of isolated events"; critical success factors to a project post-mortem they say include an open and forgiving corporate culture. Ayas and Zenuik (2001) cite psychological safety as an important factor, and for von Zedtwitz (2002), two of the four barriers to success are psychological and team-based shortcomings. On the more positive side, von Krogh (1998) says that the key enabler is care, which brings trust, empathy, and lenience in judgment, etc. Barker and Neailey (1999) call for an inclusive process, team (not individual) learning, supporting the learner, not stifling creative thinking, and setting and communicating a powerful context for the review.

The literature in the previous paragraph started to touch upon cognitive elements within the team members from whom lessons are being gathered. At a basic level, analysis can be biased by the manager or researcher's beliefs and values or by available data (Liu and Walker 1998). But there are a number of other more subtle factors, of which three are worth noting.

- The most well-known of these is perhaps hindsight bias: Bukszar and Connolly (1988) showed that even trained people could not ignore what they had been told about the actual results of a choice when evaluating decisions (Busby [1999a] also notes the issue of hindsight bias).

- Brown and Jones (1998) showed that individuals tend to attribute blame for failure either on inevitability (particular events that made failure unavoidable) or conspiracy (deliberate actions of other participants); no allowance is made for unintended consequences (denial of agency).

- Brown (2004) points to the mind-set generated by the existence of standard accepted project-management practices, showing for one case discussed that it: "need not have unfolded this way . . . It is clear that in this case the formative context had an 'aura of naturalness' (Ciborra and Lanzara) to the team members, thus blocking their learning and making them blind to any alternative"; the use of formalizations (e.g., the well-known PMBOK) means that workers understand the meanings of their actions embedded within the formalizations; the formative context is set up by following standard "best practice" (such as Bodies of Knowledge) (see also Williams [2005] and the previous discussion of Hodgson [2002]). (von Krogh [1998] in a more general setting also states that the first barriers in an organization are the need for a language, habits, formal procedures, and company paradigms.)

Formal procedures are often cited as being important to collecting lessons. In 1996, Cooke-Davies (1996) said "There is some indication that incorporating a formal process for learning pays off handsomely, but it is, as yet, based on insufficient evidence to be at all reliable," but perhaps more evidence is available now. Arthur et al. (2001) stressed the need to organize for knowledge capture. Lilly and Porter (2003) called for formal review processes and said that formal reviews were more effective than informal reviews. Styhre et al. (2004) called for more formal meetings. Schindler and Eppler (2003) claimed two reasons for not learning lessons were "lacking knowledge of project debriefing methods" and "lacking enforcement of the procedures in project manuals." Neale and Letza's (1996) advice included that an organization should have clear procedures. Pitagorsky (2000) said that one problem was workers not knowing how to go about learning lessons. (Styhre, Josephson, and Knauseder [2004] suggest introducing the role of knowledge broker.)

It is important to have a cross-section of people available when collecting lessons (Williams et al. [2005]), with formal meetings between different groups and across different phases (Styhre et al. [2004]), and obtaining multiple perspectives, involving, for example, someone external to the team (Lilly and Porter [2003]). Cicmil (2005) said that projects can only be understood by looking at a number of perspectives simultaneously: context, content, organizational behavior, communication processes, and project congruence. He presents a framework based on these to help reflect on projects and helps us to think about what knowledge is needed, as these have five different ontologies.

Two last key success factors for the process given by Schindler and Eppler (2003) not already covered previously are:

- perform the lessons learned gathering graphically, and

- strive to gain a commitment in the sense of action consequences from the gathered insights.

2.6 Transferring Knowledge

2.6.1 Organizational Learning and Knowledge Management in Projects

We looked at how organizations learn in general. How do they learn specifically from projects? How does knowledge created get distributed around the organization? This section will look at these questions, when they are not covered elsewhere in the report. It is also worth noting that Bosch-Sijtsema (2002) give a good literature review of knowledge transfer, and Morris and Loch (2004a) include a literature review of best practices in organizational learning through projects.

The first question that needs to be considered is whether the knowledge to be transferred is explicit modifiable information, or tacit personal knowledge. Carrillo (2004) points out the need to separate explicit and tacit knowledge, as IT-based and people-based methods are more appropriate, respectively. Ancori et al. (2000) (quoted in Prencipe and Tell [2001]) describe two extreme views: "all knowledge can be codified" and "all codified knowledge requires tacit knowledge to be useful." How knowledge is passed around depends upon which of these is believed and which is more appropriate to the particular circumstances. Different techniques for these different circumstances will be looked at in Section 2.6.2 (particularly looking at the work of Brady et al. [2002] and Prencipe and Tell [2001]). Hansen et al. (1999) similarly found two distinct strategies in how consulting firms managed knowledge: codification and personalization, and claimed that firms had to do predominately one or the other (e.g., 80% codification/20% personalization). Firms that tried to do both would run into trouble for various reasons (they suggested questions to help choose a strategy, such as: Do you offer standardized or customized products? Do you have a mature or innovative product? Do your people rely on explicit or tacit knowledge?

Bredillet (2004a, 2004b) put this into a wider philosophical framework, contrasting two views: *(a)* a positivist epistemology, mainly acting in operations, managing knowledge in a Western approach, using codification and explicit knowledge, based on single-loop organizational learning, where knowledge is seen as cumulative, against *(b)* a constructivist epistemology, mainly acting in projects, managing knowledge with a "Japanese" approach, using personalization and implicit knowledge, dialectical, using double-loop organizational learning, based on knowledge assets and change.

Kasvi et al. (2003) suggest that all projects have four outputs: *(a)* a product or service, *(b)* technical knowledge, *(c)* procedural knowledge about the product, and *(d)* project knowledge. Based on this theory, they discuss knowledge management strategies, both codification strategies (both the system [traditional and new technologies] and the memory itself [explicit and declarative knowledge]) and personalization strategies (again the system [memory representation, personal interactions] and the memory itself [tacit and procedural knowledge]). From this, two documents result: "The *Project Plan* can be seen as a repository for 'hard' project knowledge including project definition, activities and results. The *Team Contract* contains organizational knowledge like experiences and capitalization of lessons learned. When both are managed systematically, the project learns."

Formal IT techniques for transferring knowledge appear to be beneficial, at least for transferring explicit knowledge. Liebowitz (2005) gives a good introduction to knowledge management in projects, focusing in particular on NASA's lessons learned information system. Karni and Gordon (2000) give a classification of knowledge and propose a software model for its storage and retrieval. To research the merits of such a system, Liebowitz and Megbolugbe (2003) provide an instrument for measuring knowledge-sharing effectiveness (using a questionnaire based on communication flow, the knowledge-management environment, organizational facilitation, and measurement).

The exchange of tacit information is clearly more difficult. *A Guide to the Project Management Body of Knowledge (PMBOK® Guide)*—Third Edition (Project Management Institute 2004) is clear in some areas of knowledge management, particularly concerning explicit knowledge, but it fails to give guidance on tacit knowledge held by team members (Reich and Wee [2004]). Desouza (2003) calls for work on "facilitating tacit knowledge exchange," but his key lessons are simply the importance of top management support, the need to communicate vision, and to 'let nature takes its course' (i.e., be liberal about what can go into the database). It is not clear that this explains how to disseminate tacit knowledge. It is clear that the exchange of tacit knowledge is important in project-oriented organizations. Lindqvist, Söderlund, and Frohm (2002) looked at the generation and transfer of knowledge within three project-based organizations. In all three organizations, the transfer of knowledge relied on connecting people when problems occur through formal or informal networks, in preference to accessing their formal reports or databases. Bresnen et al. (2002) highlight the particular difficulties of knowledge capture and transfer for process rather than product innovation: "While the development of product innovations is well recorded through various design iterations and artifacts, process innovation is less likely to leave such a trail and more likely to generate tacit or procedural knowledge." Schoeniger (2005) also stresses the importance of people in knowledge-management (networks, experts passing on knowledge by teaching others, and so on).

For Koskinen (2004), the explicit/tacit dimension is one of two dimensions of knowledge in projects: tacit/explicit and additive/substitutive. *Additive,* in this case, means learning to do things better (incremental); *substitutive* means learning to do better things (discontinuous learning). He points to important differences in the ways in which knowledge is transferred. While IT-based methods are fine for additive and explicit knowledge-based projects (e.g., house building), for substitutive and tacit knowledge-based projects (e.g., product development) knowledge needs to be produced through face-to-face interactions. The explicit/tacit dimension is one of the eight "knowledge dimensions" devised by Kamara, Anumba, and Carrilo (2002) as a framework to help organizations think through knowledge management issues, the others being criticality, discipline/project based, rate of change, external/internal, shared-ness, specificity, and learning by training/interaction.

Morris and Loch (2003, 2004a, 2004b), in their empirical work, found a bias toward socialization as the preferred knowledge mode, and found this bias to be particularly strong in construction companies. They suggest a bias therefore towards learning and sense-making by narratives rather than decomposition into explicit knowledge, and that best practice should tend more in this direction (see the discussion on narratives in Section 2.5.2). They do not see a balanced set of knowledge conversion processes as being the most appropriate; rather, because of the nature of projects, "socialization would seem to be the bedrock" (Morris and Loch [2004a]).

A distinction between the processes of learning by absorption and learning by reflection needs to be made. Scarbrough et al. (2004a), talking about *learning by absorption*, note ". . . the importance of the distribution of prior and common knowledge in influencing both the scope and extent of learning within organizations. In particular. . .the structural distribution of prior and common knowledge, particularly the depth and degree of specialization and the links between different sub-units, is likely to be a crucial determinant of the transfer of [project-based learning] from its original locus to other settings." In a case study of learning in three projects within the same organization, they found that each process created different effects over the life cycle of the project. Looking at the interplay between learning (by reflection and absorption) and existing stocks of knowledge, they concluded that, for learning by absorption, prior knowledge supported learning initially but later became a constraint: "the availability of prior knowledge was increasingly seen as inhibiting the scope for learning at project level by encouraging the project team to remain within the boundaries of proven solutions." For *learning by reflection*, diversity of prior knowledge was initially a barrier but later a stimulus to reflective learning. Interestingly, they also found that the more successful the learning, the harder it was to transfer to others outside the project team (new knowledge was specific, novel, and of uncertain relevance, requiring prior knowledge to absorb).

The organizational structure is clearly key in promoting organizational learning and transfer of knowledge. Cassells (1999) warns against good post-project audits that are left "on the shelf" and emphasizes the need to change formal structures to allow information and learning to flow more freely across the organization. Reger and von Wichert-Nick (1997) show that the structure and culture of an organization are important factors in determining how effectively it can learn, and conclude that organizational learning needs: *(a)* hierarchy-free communication and flow of information, *(b)* a primary structure that is hierarchical and a secondary structure that is "supra-hierarchical and coordination-oriented," *(c)* a culture that supports teamwork, and *(d)* a culture that supports experimentation and is open to risks. Lytras and Pouloudi (2003) say that "A knowledge and learning management infrastructure is required in order to realize every knowledge organization as a learning organization capable of exploiting the organizational knowledge wealth."

The mismatch between project-orientation and long-term organizational learning was discussed in Section 2.2. Hobday (2000) compared project-based and functional/matrix structures for carrying out projects and concluded that organizational learning, both formal and informal, was better in the functional matrix structure. In the project-based division, there was little incentive or structure for learning and so many of the learning activities didn't happen: staff training younger staff, sharing lessons between projects, and completing post-project reviews. The management was able to address some of these issues by allocating time for learning/training/reflection/post-project reviews and creating more formal and informal opportunities for learning (e.g., mentoring). Stephens et al. (1999) found that it was harder to communicate lessons learned in cross-functional teams, and in a case study in a pharmaceutical company, they had to establish alternate learning structures. On the other hand, Ayas (1996), based on action research in an aircraft manufacturing company, proposed structuring projects using an information-based approach instead of traditional project-management methods. Because knowledge creation and a good exchange of information is needed to increase learning capabilities in project management, she proposed a project network structure consisting of two or three layers of cross-functional, self-managing teams, with each team leader participating as a member of the team at a higher layer; project work would be broken down into discrete modules and assigned to teams, knowledge would be created within each team (helped by their broad knowledge base), and information would be exchanged by the leaders (teams would be reconstituted for different projects to enhance the process). Bresnen, Goussevskaia, and Swan (2004) discuss the contradiction between short-term aims of projects and long-term aim of organizational learning and say that to look at the diffusion of knowledge one must consider the interaction with the ongoing project working practices. Their paper uses "structuration theory" so new project-management knowledge is derived not only from structural conditions (rules, resources, etc.) but also "from how actors make sense of and enact the system or practice, which depends upon their use of particular interpretive schemes, how they deploy particular sources of power, and how sanctioning occurs in accordance with specific norms. Consequently, it becomes important to understand the interactions between key structural features of project-based organizations, on the one hand and localized project-based working practices on the other." They also note that knowledge management will depend on the degree of projectization of the firm (pure project firms will be different from matrix, and these will be different from functional organizations that just work on occasional projects).

Just as we mentioned for systems on managing explicit knowledge, it would be useful to measure how good organizational learning is. Naot and Popper (2004) give one attempt to define the "quality" of organizational learning based on a study of four post-project reviews in the Israel Defense Forces. Using Lipshitz, Popper, and Friedman's (2002) model, they found 22 indicators summarized as: *outcomes* (which stresses the importance of assimilating lessons learned), *processes* (systematic, embedded in a culture of learning, etc.), and *immediate context* (receptive and supportive leadership that induces psychological safety). One of their reviews involved a fatality, and one year later a similar fatality occurred because of a failure to implement lessons learned. They also discuss assimilation, which is critical for organizational learning quality; the litmus test distinguishes between assimilation of lessons learned and short-term implementation as the former "tests both their suitability to the unit's operational requirements and their ability to withstand changes in personnel." Further, Terrell (1999) says if action isn't taken once lessons have been learned—they become simply lessons observed. He describes the establishment of a lessons learned program as a subproject of the main project, administered by a member of the management team but with responsibility for implementation falling on the whole management team. This offered a structured way of capturing, documenting, and acting on lessons learned, which Terrell claims gave immediate and quantifiable benefits.

2.6.2 **Practices for Distributing Lessons**

Section 2.5.1 looked at practices for collecting lessons and creating knowledge as a first step; this section looks at practices for disseminating knowledge once established. Much of this literature has already been covered; this section gives some additional points.

The obvious method is the use of a database of lessons learned. This is assumed in many papers and is clearly appropriate for capturing explicit knowledge. The most well-known lessons learned database is NASA's (NASA [2004]). Besner and Hobbs's (2004) survey of project management practice found that the use of a "database of lessons learned" differed significantly between organizations judged as low and high in project-management maturity. Databases also come first in the list of "retention practices" listed by Keegan and Turner (2001), along with reviews, training programs, competence models, learning resource centers, the intranet, quality procedures/process documentation/standards, and centers of excellence.

Clearly, the simple existence of a database is not sufficient. According to Lilly and Porter (2003), dissemination is difficult and lessons learned need to be captured in a simple manner that can be understood by people not familiar with the project. This means that lessons learned that are stored in a database should be easy to retrieve—it is not enough just to prescribe new procedures in manuals—the benefits and costs should be presented. Bullard (2005) emphasizes "pushing" information out to the organization through web-based training, revisions to process templates, audits of active project documentation, and so on. Of course there are more traditional ways of taking knowledge out. BP's post-project appraisal unit, says Gulliver (1987), distributes results by reports and booklets; Garvin (1993) talks about reports, tours, staff transfers, etc.; Gibson and Pfautz's discussion (1999) of SmithKline Beecham project review processes covers "mentors."

Following the discussion in Section 2.6.1, the use of groups of people either sharing knowledge or specific sub-groups as conduits of this knowledge is clearly important. The first of these will be discussed in Section 2.6.4 on Communities of Practice. An example of the second would be Hewlett-Packard's project management initiative group, which acts as a conduit for success stories and best practices (Englund and Graham [1999]).

Again, for an entire landscape of the methods available, we can turn to the work of Brady et al. (2002) and Prencipe and Tell (2001), both drawing on the work of Zollo and Winter (2002). These papers give organizational learning mechanisms displayed in a matrix, with differentiation between circumstances relying on people-embedded knowledge, based on a knowledge articulation process, or using ICT to support learning. Brady et al. (2002) also suggest that there could be a relationship between the learning practices used and particular characteristics of a project, namely technical complexity, technical novelty, project timing, organizational size, style of project organization, and project staffing.

These individual techniques are not independent. Eppler and Sukowski (2000) describe a layered approach to knowledge management ranging from the communications infrastructure to the shared norms, rules, and conventions, then to knowledge management processes (auditing, development, updating, and reviewing of team knowledge), tools, and techniques (although only a few techniques are mentioned in this paper) and finally leadership commitment.

Bosch-Sijtsema (2002) discusses knowledge management in virtual organizations, looking at a case study of three projects operating in (moderately) virtual organizations, each a cooperative project between non-virtual organizations. He found that "a virtual organization is not very suitable for transferring and storing organizational knowledge, however, knowledge is more transferred to the involvees (mother companies and service companies) and to (future) virtual projects." He claims therefore that, rather than trying to bring about organizational learning, virtual organizations should focus on transferring knowledge back to the non-virtual partner organizations, for example through personal expertise, social network, seminars, workshops, and formal documents.

In terms of technical systems built, Weiser and Morrison (1998) give a technical description of a "project memory" IS system and a prototype, which appeared to get user satisfaction. Tacla and Barth's (2003) give a technical description of a knowledge management system for lessons learned in R&D projects, which is multi-agent, as they say this is more appropriate for supporting knowledge creation. More generally, as mentioned in 2.5.1, Venugopal and Baets (1995) look at how IT tools, or intelligent support systems, can support organizational learning (as seen in 1995). They describe different learning processes (learning through cases, participative strategy formation, sharing individual knowledge, and exploratory knowledge) and the IT tools that can support them (database, group decision support system, cognitive mapping, and artificial neural networks).

2.6.3 Facilitating Factors and Hindrances

The literature gives various pieces of advice on what inhibits the distribution of lessons learned and organizational learning, or conversely what facilitates them. Much of this advice has been covered above, but this section tries to draw the remaining advice together.

As discussed in Section 2.2, the very temporary nature of projects inhibits learning. Koskinen, Pihlanto, and Vanharanta (2003) discuss difficulties in sharing tacit knowledge in project organizations, such as the lack of time to develop trust in temporary organizations, issues about the use of language, and benefits of colocation. As discussed by Scarbrough et al. (2004b), projects sit outside the mainstream organizational structures. This autonomy helps develop practices but inhibits flow to other parts of the organization; high levels of learning generated by overcoming knowledge boundaries produce new shared practices at project level, but then these reinforce the division between project practices and practices elsewhere in the organization, thus limiting transfer of learning—a "learning boundary." (Although, after a discussion of communities of practice [see Section 2.6.4], they comment that projects which challenge "divisions of practice" promote learning through developing new shared practice.) Bresnen, Goussevskaia, and Swan's (2004) paper using "structuration theory" notes in general that "there are a number of features related to project-based organization, namely, decentralization, the short-term emphasis on project performance and distributed work practices, which have an important bearing on the shaping and embedding of new management practice . . . the circumstances of project-based organization create their own logic of action that poses particular problems for the embedding of knowledge associated with new management practice." Morris (2002) points to a number of reasons why organizational learning and knowledge management are difficult in projects (such as supply chain patterns and procurement practices, problems of measuring performance in projects, etc.). He also points out, however, that projects have a strong process basis (e.g., gate review process), which offers particular strengths and opportunities for organizational learning.

Information technology (IT) is often seen as fundamental to knowledge management, so poor IT is sometimes blamed for inadequacy in transferring knowledge. Levene and Gale (2000) suggest there are four key enablers to learning, of which one is IT systems. In Carrillo and others' (2004) survey of construction management, 49% cited "poor IT infrastructure" as a main barrier to learning. As we have seen, the use of IT is only one part of the process of knowledge management, and a number of authors comment on the dangers of over-reliance on IT. Storey and Barnett (2000) warn implementers to "be alert to the potential differences between a paradigm which is IT-led and infused with priorities relating to knowledge capture, archiving and mining, and one based on the learning organization concept which may be inspired by wide developmental values." Anderson (2000) (cited in Bresnen et al. [2002]) says that the use of IT systems may link geographically diverse teams but may inhibit knowledge transfer if it becomes a substitute for face-to-face interaction. Newell (2004) discusses the limits of relying on IT to capture and share learning.

Two of the most important elements facilitating or hindering the transfer of knowledge are the same two key aspects mentioned in Section 2.5.4: the *structure* and the *culture* of the organization. We will look at these two in more depth.

As mentioned previously, Cassells (1999) warns against good post-project audits that are left "on the shelf" and suggests that organizations need to change their formal structures to allow information and learning to flow more freely across the organization. Sense and

Antoni (2003) carried out an empirical study and found six key factors impacting learning, three within projects and three between projects; the latter three were organizational structures between projects (the more projectized the company, the less facilitating this is), inter-project assimilation practices, and the relationship with other projects (particularly sharing people).

Scarbrough et al. (2004a) found a number of organizational factors that influence learning: project team autonomy, co-location and socialization, and "batching" of projects. In one case, project members had a greater incentive to learn as they stood to benefit directly. It was suggested that the members were able to do so because the project team became a "quasi-organization" capable of providing a shared context with its own share of prior knowledge, thereby enabling better absorption. Scarbrough et al. consider the processes of learning-by-absorption and learning-by-reflection. Regarding learning by absorption, they note "In particular,. . .the structural distribution of prior and common knowledge, particularly the depth and degree of specialization and the links between different sub-units, is likely to be a crucial determinant of the transfer of project-based learning from its original locus to other settings." (Similarly, one of the ten facilitating factors for organizational learning given by Nevis et al. [1995] and subsequently DiBella and Nevis [1998] was the "systems perspective," but they note that this was relatively lacking, and not helped by organizational structures that have strong boundaries between functions). Osterloh and Frey (2000) focus on tacit knowledge and ask "which organizational form is most conducive to knowledge generation and transfer?" and in the process identify the kinds of motivation required for the generation and transfer of tacit knowledge. Motivation is subdivided into intrinsic and extrinsic and, in particular, the "crowding effect" is used to explain behavior in transfer of knowledge.

Within the organizational structure, "for learning to become organizational, there must be roles, functions, and procedures that enable organizational members to systematically collect, analyze, store, disseminate, and use information relevant to their own and other members' performance" say Lipshitz, Popper, and Friedman (2002), who use the term *organizational learning mechanisms* to mean "observable organizational subsystems in which organization members interact for the purpose of learning."

There are also a number of specific individual aspects of the organization. Carmona and Grönlund's (1998) study found three aspects of the organizational structure that affected whether learning was sustained: (*a*) strict budgeting can constrain implementation of learning, (*b*) the teams have to be recognized by the rest of the organization, and (*c*) the benefits of a reward system (both intrinsic and extrinsic). Harris (2002) suggested that one reason why lessons were rarely learned was because of a "gulf" between technical and business areas.

The project team itself also has a structure. Sense (2003a) gives five structural attributes that support learning in project teams: learning relationships, understanding cognitive styles, knowledge management within and external to the project team, learning environment (organization support for learning), and authority to learn. Edmondson (2002) says that "Laboratory studies of group learning found that stable membership promotes learning and tacit coordination" (e.g., Moreland and Argote [1998]). This is contrary to the normal assumption in project management, as it is assumed that project teams start fresh on each project. Edmondson's research included the identification of different patterns of team learning based on levels of reflection and also tried to explain the observed difference in team learning, power, and perceptions of interpersonal risk being identified as the key factors in understanding these differences.

The study of the social processes underlying learning is important because of the importance of the organizational structure. Bresnen et al. (2003) point to the importance of social and behavioral processes in both capturing and transferring knowledge. Bresnen et al. (2002) say that any of the barriers to learning are social (organizational and behavioral), which are not addressed by current knowledge management approaches. This leads us from the organizational structure to the underlying organizational culture.

In Carrillo and others' (2004) construction management survey, 76% cited "organizational culture" as a main barrier to learning. One of Levene and Gale's (2000) four key enablers to learning was "culture and environment."

Lipshitz, Popper, and Friedman's (2002) study of culture developed five values that promote productive learning:

- Transparency (the willingness to expose one's thoughts and actions to others in order to receive feedback),

- Integrity (the willingness to seek and provide info regardless of its implications),

- Issue-orientation (focusing on the relevance of information to the issue under consideration regardless of the social standing or rank of source or recipient),

- Inquiry (persisting in investigation until full understanding is achieved), and

- Accountability (willingness to assume responsibility for learning and implementation of lessons learned).

In Sense and Antoni's (2003) empirical study noted previously, the three key factors impacting learning from within projects were:

- Individual authority level (the ways in which authority differences can hinder learning),

- Project sponsor actions (the project sponsor being generally more interested in project output), and

- Organizational environment influences (which can be positive and negative)

(One organization provided learning forums; prioritization comes from the organization.)

One factor highlighted in Carmona and Grönlund's (1998) study of two European car manufacturers found that high-power distance (the dependence on relationships among people) and high uncertainty avoidance in Spain (compared to Sweden) meant that middle managers had less responsibility and less decision-making power, so are less able to implement changes. Similar differences between two cultures arose in Kidd's (1998) study of knowledge creation in Japanese manufacturing companies in Italy (based on Nonaka's SECI model), with facilitating factors being training by the donor company (sending Italians to the parent company in Japan), opportunities for peer group discussion, empowerment at the local level (not just compliance), appreciation of tacit knowledge held by receiving company, and good exchange of data. Hindrances included elitism, rigid processes, and systems.

Two other aspects of the organizational culture are important:

- *Openness*. Huber (1999) says that an organizational culture is needed when free and full knowledge is actively pursued as a matter of course. Similarly, one of Nevis and others' (1995) (subsequently DiBella and Nevis [1998]) ten facilitating factors is a climate of openness.

- *Desire to learn*. Harris (2002) claims that one of the reasons lessons are rarely learned is because of reliance upon existing routines (the prevailing organizational systems actually encouraging conformity and stability rather than learning). Cooke-Davies (1996) identifies three characteristics necessary for organizational learning: *(a)* a focus/culture of searching for improvement, *(b)* a structured process that challenges the status quo, and *(c)* skills to learn and a habit of facilitated dialogue. Gann and Salter (2000) point to problems of capturing and transferring knowledge through the organization partly due to the discontinuous and temporary nature of projects as discussed in 2.2.2, but also to a reluctance to seek out lessons learned in the construction industry, which rewards novelty rather than standardization.

Different policies are suitable for different circumstances and organizations, but some authors have pointed to particular management policies. For example, five of Huber's (1999) ten facilitating factors to help team learning are:

- Staffing practice, that is, using people well networked in the technical community

- Institutionalized practice of sharing and explicating evolving knowledge within the team and examining it,

* Institutionalized practice of the team's creating and delivering a lessons learned file,

* A practice of transferring a member of the knowledge-generating team into a new team to find out what the first team learned,

* A practice of identifying the member of a need-to-know unit who seems to have the most acceptable absorptive capacity to use as a knowledge conduit and disseminator.

Levene and Gale's (2000) key enablers to learning include management systems, that is, methods and procedures such as post-project reviews and learning histories.

Top management support is important in all knowledge management initiatives (Storey and Barnett [2000]) but particularly in encouraging a culture of learning, motivating members of the organization to invest in sharing lessons, and in seeking learning. (Newell [2004] points out the issue that project teams often only seek help when they perceive a need.) In Fong's (2005) survey of knowledge management among quantity surveyors in Hong Kong and the UK, the most critical factor for knowledge management success was found to be top management support, followed by employee participation. Other similar motivational factors are highlighted by a number of authors. Hall and Sapsed (2005) ask what motivates people to share knowledge, and develop a 2x2 matrix based on *control mechanisms* (mechanistic or social, the latter getting employees' preferences to coincide with those of management) versus *motivation* (extrinsic, i.e., pay for performance, or intrinsic, i.e., for satisfaction). Gann and Salter (2000), note problems with capturing and transferring knowledge through the organization due to a reluctance to seek out lessons learned in the construction industry, which rewards novelty rather than standardization.

Organizational politics also affects motivation and the ability to learn. Sense (2003b) divides learning into four types with a 2x2 matrix depending on the sources being formal or informal, and the project manager's political approach being influencing or accommodating. These four types of learning are purposeful, networked, adaptive, and opportunistic. Bourne and Walker (2004) also emphasize that, as well as hard and soft skills, project managers need to have a good understanding of organizational politics in order for a project to succeed. Oshri (2000) highlights (among other problems) tensions between knowledge transfer and expertise development. However, while these motivational factors are certainly important, it should be noted that Szulanski (1996) claims that "contrary to conventional wisdom that places primary blame on motivational factors, the major barriers to internal knowledge transfer are shown to be knowledge-related factors such as the recipient's lack of absorptive capacity, causal ambiguity, and an arduous relationship between the source and the recipient." He concludes that incentives alone are inadequate for driving knowledge transfer, and the organization needs to understand systematically and communicate practices.

Finally, a few other comments are made in the literature on aspects of facilitating or hindering learning:

* One of Levene and Gale's (2000) four key enablers to learning is "metrics," which can help promote learning.

* Busby (1999b) looks at dissemination to other projects, reporting that in one review, managers of new projects (outsiders) were invited to attend the review—he suggests that dissemination this way is more effective than using written summaries.

* Stephens et al. (1999), when talking about cross-functional teams, say that teams are reluctant to adopt best practices from elsewhere in the organization because of concern about meeting timelines.

* Lynn, Reilly, and Akgun (2000) carried out a large study of NPD teams and found two forms of learning: information acquisition (capturing information) and information implementation (the productive use of information). The key factors were vision clarity, vision stability, vision support, recording (which is both a product and a process), reviewing, and filing. All of these things positively impact team learning, albeit through somewhat indirect paths.

2.6.4 **Communities of Practice**

It has been emphasized above that much of the knowledge sharing process is a social, inter-personal process. We have said, for example, that information on its own does not create knowledge; we need to develop communities who think together (McDermott [1999]). There have been various models of how this could or should operate, but one particular model that has become in favor in recent years is that of the "Communities of Practice" (CoP for this section), based on the ideas particularly of Wenger (1998).

These are communities of interest that cut across project teams and enable sharing within the permanent organization, partly overcoming the problems related to the temporary nature of projects. (Hence Garrety, Robertson, and Badham's [2004] promotion of the idea of CoPs to accumulate knowledge and bring it to [temporary] projects.) Swan, Scarbrough, and Robertson (2002), looking at the use of CoPs in the management of innovation, use Lave and Wenger's (1991) definition of a CoP and emphasize that ". . . the defining feature of communities of practice (as opposed to, say, project teams) is that they are seen to emerge spontaneously from the (largely informal) networking among groups of individuals who have similar work-related activities and interests. . . . Organizations are depicted as embracing multiple and heterogeneous communities of practice, and communities of practice may span organizations." As well as a general discussion on the power, manageability, and limitations of CoPs, this particular article used the case of a prostate cancer therapy project and found that the project team employed a "rhetorical strategy," which helped to forge coordinating links across networks and communities and also facilitated new encounters between existing groups in the field. Similar discussion occurs in the work of Lesser and Prusak (2000), who look at the role of CoPs in the processes of creating, sharing, and applying organizational knowledge.

The bringing together of personnel seems to reflect the way that learning actually happens in projects. Styhre et al. (2004) claimed that most learning in the Swedish construction industry happened through informal discussion with others. They state that culture is oral; people learn through mentoring, discussing practical problems, storytelling, and communities of practice, though this means learning is hard to manage. When Lindqvist, Söderlund, and Frohm (2002) looked at the generation and transfer of knowledge within three project-based organizations, they noted that the transfer of knowledge for each organization relied on connecting people when problems occur through formal or informal networks, in preference to accessing the organizations' formal reports or databases. Brown and Duguid (1991) take these ideas and show how they lead to structures such as CoPs. They say that traditional models of working and learning are flawed because: *(a)* the way people actually work usually differs fundamentally from the way in which organizations formally describe that work (i.e., there is noncanonical as well as canonical practice); and *(b)* learning happens not just by transmitting explicit knowledge but also by acquiring tacit knowledge within a communal context. In practice people form informal communities of practice which are "often noncanonical and not recognized by the organization. They are more fluid and interpenetrative than bounded, often crossing the restrictive boundaries of the organization to incorporate people from outside . . . And significantly, communities are emergent. That is to say their shape and membership emerges in the process of activity, as opposed to being created to carry out a task." (Orr's [1990] account of photocopy machine repairmen is used as an example.)

There are a number of accounts of actual communities of practice. As a few examples: Steichen (2001) describes how Boeing formally established a CoP for project management. The survey in construction management conducted by Carrillo et al. (2004) showed that 43% of large companies and 7% of small companies had used CoPs. Delisle (2004) reports that the Canadian government encourages the development and growth of CoPs by creating the appropriate culture and structures.

It should be said, though, that Scarbrough et al. (2004b) point out that projects sit outside of the mainstream organizational structures. This autonomy helps develop practices but inhibits flow to other parts of the organization. High levels of learning generated by overcoming knowledge boundaries produce new shared practices at the project level, but then these reinforce the division between project practices and practices elsewhere in the organization, thereby limiting the transfer of learning—a "learning boundary." They go on to say that CoPs in stable organizational contexts help learning but form a barrier to transferring learning in other contexts. Project work tends to be more specific and contingent than what CoPs do.

The idea of CoPs can in fact be taken beyond the individual organization. A prime example of this is the "network of 15 blue-chip organizations from a variety of organizations that have been working together . . . to identify and benchmark 'best project management practice'" (Cooke-Davies [1996]). Another example is the study by Cooke-Davies where he looks at how practices in project management differ between industries, carried out for a CoP of project managers in the pharmaceutical industry (Cooke-Davies and Arzymanow [2002]).

2.7 Case Studies

We have identified a number of case studies in this chapter. Much of the work reported has been based on empirical work in real cases. The nature of the work is that while much is positivist, quantitative work, in order to understand the complexities of the operations of human-based organizations, much of the work has been based on large phenomenological studies of cases. Some of these companies are not identified, but we have looked at Gulliver's (1987) well known report of BP's post project appraisal unit, as well as Brander-Löf, Hilger, and André's (2000) description of a procedure for lessons learned developed at Ericsson; Englund and Graham's (1999) experience with Hewlett-Packard; Crosman's (2002) experience with the U.S. Army; Gibson and Pfautz's (1999) experience at SmithKline Beecham; and Stephens and others' (1999) work with Eli Lilly. We referred to NASA methods (see also Paté-Cornell and Dillon 2001) and noted a number of other case studies in this chapter.

Learning comes from good and poor experiences (e.g., Pan and Flynn's [2003] account of a failed project in a Japanese organization gives useful learning). This also applies to establishing lessons learned programs. A poor experience of trying to implement post-project reviews was given by Rasper, Stanier, and Carluccio (2002) in MDS Sciex, because post-mortem contributions were only from latter phases of the project and had poor focus. In this case, there were too many disciplines involved, information was gathered but never used, there was no follow-up, and the process focused on data collection but did not address how to learn from this. The company has now improved the quality of the data by holding post-mortems with the right people at the end of each phase, with other improvements including setting organizational priorities and establishing a process for implementing solutions and tracking progress.

The film industry is an interesting example of project management in general. The industry is entirely project based; and learning happens by individuals and the industry at large rather than by any permanent organization, say DeFillippi and Arthur (1998), who observed the making of a Hollywood film by the independent film-making industry. The industry learns while participant firms come and go. DeFillippi (2001) cites the industry as an example where "the deepest learning accrues to people who assume brokering roles at the intersections of multiple communities engaged in projects requiring joint cooperation among their contributors."

There are a number of other case study reports in the literature. Landes et al. (1999) describe a case study of how organizations learn from experience based on software projects in DaimlerChrysler Corporation, using an "experience factory" approach. In relation to some of the fundamental concepts of organizational learning reflected in the literature (specifically, organizational memories, experience factories, and knowledge modeling), the paper highlights the tension that exists between "conceptual desires and pragmatic necessities." Patriotta (2003) gives a study of knowledge creation set in the context of a longitudinal study of two Fiat auto manufacturing plants, focusing on longitudinal involvement with the research settings, breakdown of routines, and the analysis of narratives. According to Patriotta, knowledge recedes into the organizational background as a result of past experience; habit; and experiential, tacit-related factors, all settling down. Looking for breakdowns or discontinuities are ways to access this learning. Terrell (1999) reports on a case study (replacing steam generators) where lessons learned were collected throughout the project life cycle and applied immediately so their value could be recognized. Establishing a lessons learned program became a subproject of the main project and was administered by a member of the management team but with responsibility for implementation falling on the whole management team.

While maybe not conventional post-project review, Popper and Lipshitz (1998) look at organizational learning mechanisms in the context of conducting after-action reviews within the Israel Defense Force Air Force. Their emphasis is on the quality of review, and they note two contributing factors: *(a)* technology to reveal error (quality improved dramatically with the introduction of video cameras in the cockpit and ground sensors), and *(b)* willingness to confront error, acquired through the process of socialization into the air force. This latter cultural facet of learning was mentioned in Section 2.6.4 previously. (Their paper [Lipshitz, Popper, and Oz 1996] reports on introducing a lessons learning system to the Israel Defense Force; Naot and Popper [2004] draw some generic lessons from four post-project reviews.)

2.8 Conclusions

This chapter summarized the literature, therefore a summary of that would lose much of the content. However, a few overall comments can be made:

- Project reviews, or post-mortems, are very important and are an integral part of the "learning organization." Project management standards suggest that reviews should be performed during the project as well as at the conclusion, but give little guidance as to how to accomplish them.

- Project reviews are difficult, particularly because of the temporary organization aspect of projects, but also because of the complexity of projects and project organizations, and the fact that projects often don't follow a clear plan but are rather "sense-making" processes, as well as other reasons.

- There is a wealth of research and literature in the areas on knowledge (particularly tacit knowledge), personal learning, organizational learning, and knowledge management, which does not seem to have been translated into practical benefits for developing our project management methodologies. Organizational culture and organizational structure are important aspects in how organizations learn.

- There is also much literature about knowledge management, with IT solutions being considered more appropriate to managing explicit knowledge, tacit knowledge being more appropriately spread by socialization.

- The literature is divided as to whether "learning from projects" is ubiquitous or a fairly rare occurrence.

- Reflective learning diaries, recorded stories, and micro articles are used to record individual experiences. Various types of review groups, in addition to learning histories and project team meetings are used to gather group experiences. Conflicting reports from project team meetings need to be taken into account and the root causes explored. This can be at the end of the project, but also mid-project. A small group of papers set out the landscape of available techniques and look at which parts are more appropriate for which organizations.

- The social process of narrative telling and recording can be effective to explore project issues, capturing their complexity and behaviors outside of organizational norms.

- It can sometimes be important to understand the complex systemicity underlying project outcomes, and various methods have been used for this.

- The literature gives a number of techniques to support both methods of knowledge dissemination, often based around a lessons learned database. Social methods are perhaps more appropriate for tacit knowledge and IT-mediated methods for codifiable knowledge. The same small group of papers gives a landscape of available techniques.

- There is increasing interest in communities of practice for knowledge dissemination, particularly for complex or tacit knowledge.

- Lack of time and opportunity, cost considerations, and the culture and structure of the organization seem to be key inhibiting factors in collecting lessons to learn, including lack of incentives, lack of formal procedures, and cognitive issues. Similar issues inhibit knowledge transfer, but also the temporary nature of projects, poor IT infrastructure, and lack of top management support.

3
SURVEY OF PRACTICE: DO ORGANIZATIONS LEARN FROM PROJECTS?

3.1 Introduction

This chapter describes the results of the survey of project managers on the use of "lessons learned" from projects. The questionnaire was designed to answer specific questions about how project managers learn lessons from projects, and whether they consider it to be successful. The questionnaire was piloted with a small group of experienced project managers from the UK, U.S., and China, and modified using their comments. The questionnaire was then distributed by means of the Zoomerang™ website (www.zoomerang.com). There were 522 usable responses (plus 14 unusable responses).

The questionnaire consisted of five sections:

*   *Questions 1–9* looked at what organizations currently did about lessons learned (discussed in Section 3.3).

*   *Questions 10–18* looked at how successful respondents felt that organizations were in learning lessons (discussed in Sections 3.4 and 3.5).

*   *Questions 19–22* asked what respondents felt was the best practice in the lessons learned area.

*   *Questions 23–24* asked what respondents felt stopped them from doing more to learn lessons (both discussed in Section 3.6).

*   *Questions 25–32* gathered demographic information about the respondents and their organizations (discussed in Section 3.2).

Section 3.7 provides some conclusions.

The Project Management Institute, along with every project management organization within the International Project Management Association (IPMA), was approached to circulate the details of the survey to their members. Although PMI cooperated by providing the link in circulated material, many of the IPMA organizations either did not reply, refused to circulate the details due to organizational policy, or were unable to circulate the survey to their members within the few months prior to the close of the survey (the Spanish and Dutch societies being notable in their helpfulness). Due to this somewhat disappointing response from the associations, the survey response therefore was skewed towards PMI members. Of the 522 usable responses, 96% stated that they were members of PMI (although 2% were members of APM, 3% were members of an IPMA organization, 1% were members of AIPM [Australia], and 13% were members of other professional bodies [note that the possibility of multiple membership in this response exists]).

It is also clear that the survey is skewed towards those with an interest in "lessons learned" activity. One of the PMI broadcast e-mails, for example, had 15 links which readers could click; potential respondents had to click on a link entitled *Do organizations learn lessons from projects? Research survey seeks participants.* Clearly, only readers of the e-mail with an interest in this question would click on the link.

The questionnaire as posted on the Zoomerang™ website is shown in Appendix 1. The bare results reported by Zoomerang are shown in Appendix 2, and these results (plus analysis of the correlations within the data) are reported in this book. A certain amount of statistical analysis of the data was done; however, it should be noted that factor analysis did not generate any interesting results because of the colinearity of the data.

3.2 **Profile of Respondents**

This section relates to Questions 25–32 and covers the demographic profile of the respondents.

As shown in Figure 3-1, the industry most highly represented was IT (26.1%), followed by manufacturing (12.6%), finance (10.9%), and consulting/business management (10.0%). Approximately 14.7% were unspecified. Organizations varied in size from under 100 to over 100,000 employees, with 77.2% falling between those two extremes.

Not surprisingly, the respondents to this survey came from project-oriented organizations. More than one-half of the respondents (53.9%) said that their organizations do most or all of their work in a project orientation; three-quarters of the respondents (73.6%) said that 50% or more was done in a project orientation; and only a few (4.7%) said that projects arose infrequently. The mode for the average size of projects was between $100 thousand (U.S.) and $1 million (U.S.) (39.8%), with 85.0% of responses lying in the range $10 thousand to $10 million (U.S.). As shown in Figure 3-1, the maturity of project management within the organizations was described as ad hoc (8.4% of respondents), encouraged informally (26.1%), integrated into the organization's processes (41.4%), or integrated and continuously improving (24.1%). These stages of maturity align with

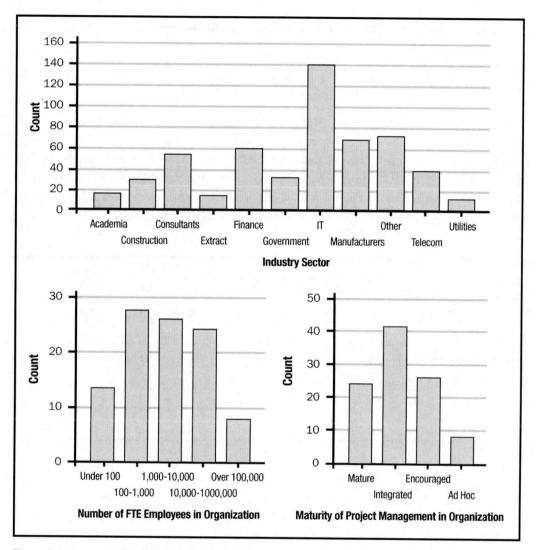

Figure 3-1 **Demographics of Respondents**

standard maturity models and are described as ad hoc, encouraged, integrated, and mature in this report.

As described in Section 3.1, the great majority of respondents are members of PMI (96%). Of the respondents, 54% have a project management qualification, of which 83% are PMP-qualified. The modal and median number of years' experience of managing projects was 5 to 10 years (36.8%).

3.3 What Are Organizations Doing?

This section covers Questions 1–9 of the questionnaire, which looked into current practices of organizations.

3.3.1 Adherence to formal procedures (Q1)

From the responses, 62.4% said their organization had formal procedures for learning lessons from projects, although of these only 11.7% said that they closely adhered to the procedures. There was a strong correlation between this variable and the maturity of project management in the organization (which is not surprising, as maturity of project management is defined by organizations having processes to carry out activities such as lessons learned). (See Table 3-1.)

Maturity	Adherence to Formal Procedures			
	Strong	Medium	Weak	None
Mature (122)	18.9	54.1	9.0	18.0
Integrated (207)	5.8	47.8	18.8	27.5
Encouraged (130)	0.8	18.5	21.5	59.2
Ad hoc (42)	0	7.1	14.3	78.6
All responses (508, which, includes 7 where maturity was not known)	7.3	38.6	16.5	37.6

Table 3-1 **Adherence to Formal Procedures Is Stronger in More Mature Organizations**

3.3.2 A Specific Department for Lessons Learned (Q2, 3)

Results from these questions revealed that 32% of the organizations have a specific department that is responsible for supporting learning from projects. The primary roles of these departments are to capture learning from projects (56%), to ensure compliance to standards (50%), to transfer learning to future departments (44%), and to audit the lessons learned process (25%).

3.3.3 Prevalence of Lessons Learned Activities (Q4, 5)

As shown in Table 3-1, the frequency with which organizations perform lessons learned activities is much greater for organizations in which project management is more mature (again, this is to some extent a truism). Note that 62.0% of organizations in which project management is mature do lessons learned after all or most projects, compared with 40.6% in which project management is integrated, and only 13.8% in which project management is encouraged or ad hoc. It should be noted that a few (seven) organizations in which project management is mature responded that they do not perform lessons learned activities.

Organizations doing lessons learned activities were coded depending upon whether they did these activities on a regular basis (either on completion of major milestones or deliverables or at regular intervals), post project only, in response to problems or business needs only ("reactive"), ad hoc only, or a combination of post-project and reactive or ad hoc ("mixed"). (A combination of reactive and ad hoc was coded as reactive.) The most widespread practice is to do lessons learned upon completion of the project only. This was reported by 51.1% of the organizations, with no significant difference between organizations of different maturities. The greatest differences arose when comparing organizations doing lessons learned at regular intervals (33.6% of mature organizations compared with 10.7% of organizations in which project management is encouraged or ad hoc), and in response to problems or business needs only (3.4% compared with 13.4%).

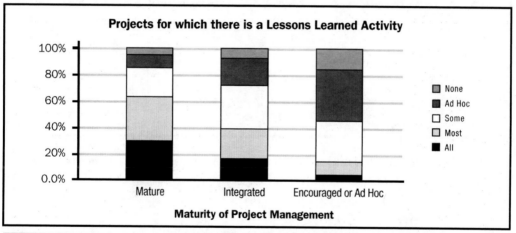

Maturity	Projects for Which There Is a Lessons Learned Activity, %				
	All	**Most**	**Some**	**Ad Hoc**	**None**
Mature (121)	29.8	32.2	22.3	9.9	5.8
Integrated (209)	16.7	23.9	30.6	21.1	7.7
Encouraged or ad hoc (160)	4.4	9.4	31.3	39.4	15.6
All responses (496, which includes 6 in which maturity is not known	15.9	21.0	29.0	24.4	9.7

Figure 3-2 **Organizations Where PM is More Mature Do Lessons Learned for More Projects**

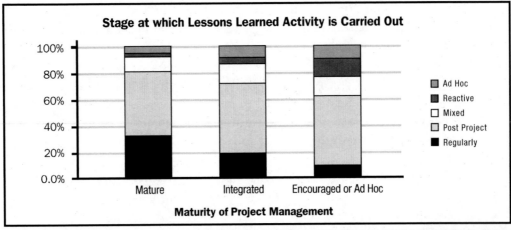

Maturity	Stage At Which Lessons Learned Activity Is Carried Out, %				
	Regularly	Post Project	Mixed	Reactive	Ad Hoc
Mature (116)	33.6	48.3	10.3	3.4	4.3
Integrated (196)	20.9	51.5	14.8	4.6	8.2
Encouraged or ad hoc (149)	10.7	51.7	14.8	13.4	9.4
All responses (468, includes 7 where maturity is not known)	20.9	51.1	13.5	7.1	7.5

Figure 3-3 **Organizations Where PM Is More Mature Are More Likely to Do Lessons Learned Regularly and Less Likely to Do It in Response to Problems or a Business Need**

3.3.4 **Who is Involved? (Q6)**

As shown in Figure 3-4, people most commonly involved in the lessons learned activities are project management staff (94.8%) and technical staff (69.9%). In most organizations (80.6%), the project management staff works alongside other staff. It is interesting to note that outside personnel are involved in lessons learned more often than might be expected from the literature—more than one-fourth of respondents (28.4%) reported customer involvement, and 15.5% reported subcontractor involvement. On the other hand, apart from project-management, senior management, and technical staff, there appears to be less of a presence of internal staff than suggested by best practices. Surprisingly, approximately only one in ten respondents reported that financial staff were involved in lessons learned, a similar number for contract/legal staff, and only 1.7% for human resource management staff.

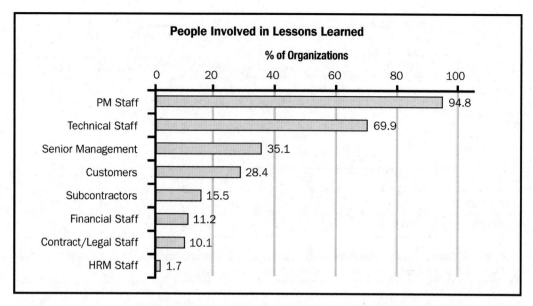

Figure 3-4 **Outsiders Are Often Involved in Lessons Learned, but Are Rarely Involved for Disciplines Other than Management/Technical**

3.3.5 **What Processes Are Organizations Using? (Q7, 8)**

Questions 7 and 8 presented the respondent with lists of processes aimed at capturing lessons and transferring them outside of the project team, which were drawn from the literature, experience, and the pilot questionnaires. For these two questions, the respondents were constrained by these lists.

To capture lessons, the processes used most often are meetings (77.8% of organizations), followed by interviews and project audits. These processes and learning diaries are used significantly more in organizations where PM is mature. For example, these organizations are nearly three times more likely to use project audits than organizations where PM is ad hoc or encouraged.

To transfer lessons, the processes most often used are written documentation, moving people, ad hoc, and presentations. Organizations where PM is mature are more likely to use all the processes listed with the exception of ad hoc processes, which they are less likely to use and moving people, where there is no relationship. The differences are particularly great for the use of a resources center, new procedures, IT-mediated methods, communities of practice, narratives, mentoring, micro articles, and training, with mature organizations more than three times as likely to use each of these than organizations where PM is ad hoc or encouraged.

	All Responses (451, includes 7 where Maturity is Not Known)	Maturity of Project Management			
		Mature (114)	Integrated (188)	Encouraged (113)	Ad Hoc (29)
Meetings*	77.8	87.7	77.1	71.7	65.5
Interviews*	30.4	40.4	30.3	23.9	13.8
Project audits*	29.3	44.7	30.9	16.8	10.3
Learning diaries*	19.5	30.7	17.6	13.3	10.3
Narratives	17.1	17.5	18.6	15.0	10.3
Ask customers	17.1	21.9	16.0	15.9	3.4
External facilitator	12.6	14.0	14.4	7.1	13.8
External team	4.4	4.4	4.3	6.2	0

* Indicates differences in use between organizations of different maturity are significant.

Table 3-2 **Percentage of Companies Using Each Process to Capture Lessons**

	All Responses (451, includes 7 where Maturity is Not Known)	Maturity of Project Management			
		Mature (113)	Integrated (179)	Encouraged (107)	Ad Hoc (26)
Documentation*	52.5	64.6	52.5	42.1	42.3
Moving people	45.8	50.4	49.2	37.4	38.5
Ad hoc*	37.0	21.2	34.1	54.2	61.5
Presentations*	26.2	29.2	30.7	18.7	11.5
IT mediated*	22.0	43.4	18.4	8.4	11.5
Mentoring*	21.1	31.9	22.3	9.3	11.5
New procedures*	17.8	35.4	16.8	5.6	3.8
Narratives*	17.1	25.7	19.6	7.5	3.8
Training*	14.4	21.2	15.6	7.5	3.8
CoP's*	11.6	20.4	11.2	4.7	3.8
Resources center*	6.0	13.3	4.5	.9	0
Micro articles*	3.0	7.1	1.1	2.8	0

* Indicates differences in use between organizations of different maturity are significant (combining figures for "ad hoc" and "encouraged" where appropriate).

Table 3-3 **Percentage of Companies Using Each Process to Transfer Lessons**

Similar differences in the use of processes can be seen between organizations having and adhering to formal procedures and those which do not, although the differences are not as great. For example 35.4% of those with formal procedures use project audits compared with 23.7% of those without, and 24.7% use learning diaries compared with 14.9% without.

3.3.6 **Sector Differences**

From Figure 3-5, at first glance it appears that there are differences in project management maturity between the different sectors, with IT, extraction, and utilities generally more mature and government and academia less mature. However, the differences are only significant for IT and government (comparing mature/integrated and encouraged/ad hoc against the mean for the group).

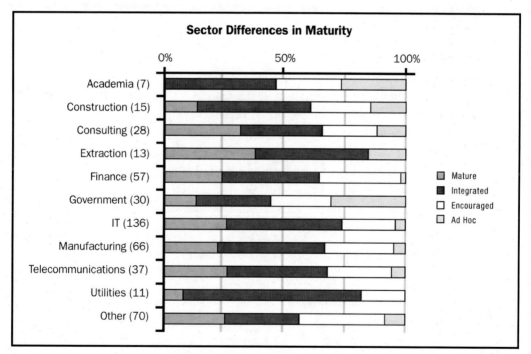

Figure 3-5 **Maturity of Project Management in Different Industries (Sample Size in Parentheses)**

As shown in Table 3-4, there are a few significant differences in the processes used by the different industries. The two most distinct industries are construction and government. Construction makes greater use of presentations and project audits and less use of mentoring than other industries, and government makes less use of IT, presentations, and project audits.

Process	Used More	Used Less
IT Mediated Methods		Government Finance
Mentoring		Construction Manufacturing
Presentations	Construction	Government
Project Audits	Construction Extraction IT	Government

Table 3-4 **Industries for Which the Use of Processes Differs Significantly from the Mean**

3.3.7 **Other Methods**

Respondents were also given the opportunity to identify methods other than the methods listed in the questionnaire. To the question which read "Are there any other ways project teams can access lessons from previous projects?" 42% of the respondents filled in something to this question, some of whom simply answered "no." A few answers gave more than one technique or tool, and these answers were split into their constituent items, leaving 175 useful answers. The majority of answers then consisted of three sets:

- Some sort of database-related answer, or a similar electronic file that could be searched—38% of the answers.

- An answer that involved asking other people who had been involved in projects—31% of the answers.

- An answer effectively describing documentation which had to be looked up—17% of answers.

There was a mixture of other answers, five regarding the revision of procedures; two discussing post-project meetings; two describing staff presentations; and two giving ideas related to communities-of-practice type organizations, others including guides, yearly evaluations, mass e-mails, expert estimation sheets, and "intranet articles" (no more details given). Four additional answers described serious attention to the lessons learned process and are given here, quoted in more detail:

- "Customer-facing project managers . . . are required to revisit lessons learned documented on previous projects that are similar in nature and interview the project manager to gain a better understanding of the challenges encountered. This becomes an agenda item in their project kick-off meeting. They are also required to revisit the risk management plan regularly and share with the appropriate team members at least monthly to ensure a common vision is shared."

* "I require that teams perform tactical walks (Start, Stop, Continue . . . Analysis) review to integrate learning on a weekly basis. These lessons are passed along by personal networking within our organization."

* "Lessons learned portfolio management. Metrics should be set with goals to reduce lessons learned in key critical areas."

* "When we do LL's [lessons learned] we end them with a list of action items so that the lessons are proactively reinforced. These items get assigned to an "owner" and a date is assigned. Periodic follow-up should be done to ensure completion of the action items and documentation of actual results."

Finally, two answers that provide examples of how frustrated some project managers clearly felt:

* "Bad press is usually the only way we get lessons learned on projects outside each silo'd project team."

* An answer not necessarily repeatable, but which involved: ". . . allowing senior managers to cry and scream until they are worn out, then reality dawns and their brains awake . . ."

3.4 How Successful Are these Processes?

This section looks at the respondents' views about how successful their organizations' processes are. It gives the results of Questions 10–18. Factors contributing to this success, that is, relationships between these answers and the data discussed previously in Sections 3.2 and 3.3, will be discussed in Section 3.5.

3.4.1 Measures of Success (Q10–12, 16–18)

Respondents were asked for their views on "How good are your processes for learning from projects?" and "How useful would you say are the lessons you learn?" The responses are provided in Table 3-5.

The greatest perceived problems relating to the success of lessons learned are getting to the root causes of project outcomes and creating knowledge rather than simply collecting data. Areas of least concern are finding lessons which are generalizable to other projects, achieving truthful outputs, and identifying clear issues.

Quality of Processes	Tend to Agree or Strongly Agree (%)
Lessons are generalizable to other projects (11b)	70.4
Outputs are truthful (11d)	68.2
We identify clear issues (10a)	67.3
We prioritize issues (10b)	58.6
We learn complex lessons (11a)	57.4
We avoid blame (10c)	57.3
People share learning about failures (10d)	57.3
We create knowledge rather than simply collecting data (11c)	44.9
We get to the root causes of project outcomes (10e)	40.5

Table 3-5 **Agreement with Statements Relating to the Quality of the Processes**

Measuring success in terms of increased competency, the benefits of doing lessons learned were perceived to accrue significantly more to the individual project managers than to the organization as a whole (see Table 3-6).

Results of Lessons Learned	Tend to Agree or Strongly Agree (%)
My competency as a project manager has increased (12c)	86.7
Project competency within the organization has increased (12b)	60.8
Projects are more successful (12a)	55.1

Table 3-6 **Agreement with Statements Relating to What the Processes Have Achieved**

The transfer of lessons within an organization appears to be one of the major difficulties of learning from projects: on every question relating to this there was stronger disagreement (that the potential benefit actually occurred) than agreement (see Table 3-7). Nearly half of respondents (47.8%) agree that the lessons learned are transferred from the individual to the project team. A much smaller percentage (35.6%) agrees that they are transferred to other project teams, and only 22.2% agree that they are transferred elsewhere in the organization. However, in 65.5% of organizations, lessons learned from projects are either sometimes or routinely implemented into the organizations' processes, and 56.9% of organizations have changed their strategy because of the lessons learned process; clearly some lessons are being learned within the organizations despite the somewhat gloomy assessment by respondents.

Transfer of Lessons Learned	Tend to Agree or Strongly Agree (%)
Lessons learned move from the individual to the project team (16a)	47.8
Lessons learned are applied by other project teams (16c)	35.6
Learning is achieved across cultures (16d)	23.0
Lessons learned move from the project team to the organization (16b)	22.2

Table 3-7 **Agreement with Statements Relating to How Well Lessons Are Transferred**

3.4.2 **Benchmarking (Q13–15)**

Only a minority of organizations use benchmarking or other ways to measure their processes for effectiveness. Of the 471 responses, 94 (20%) indicated that they use at least one way of measuring their processes (see Table 3-8).

Response	Number of Cases
Learning processes are measured for effectiveness	42
Learning processes are benchmarked	74*
Benchmark against similar projects within the organization	61
Benchmark against other organizations in the industry	26
Benchmark against organizations in other industries	11
Benchmark against dissimilar projects within the organization	10
Positive response to at least one of the above	94
*The results for Q14 ("Do you benchmark?") were adjusted to include cases with a positive response to Q15 ("if yes.").	

Table 3-8 **Responses to Questions Relating to Measuring Processes for Effectiveness**

Of the 42 responses indicating that processes were measured for effectiveness, there was little indication as to how this was done. Many answers gave little information as to the processes or measures used, and a few answered "why" *not* "how." However, it is worth noting that:

- Two replies indicated that standards such as ISO or CMMI were used.

- Seven replies described a particular process that appeared to give quantitative measures.

- Six replies described a particular process that appeared to be essentially qualitative.

- One reply indicated a third party involved in the measurement process.

3.5 Factors Contributing to the Perceived Success of Lessons Learned

This section looks at relationships between respondents' views about how successful their organizations' processes are (as described in the results of Questions 10 to 18) and the other data collected (such as those about maturity, size, and processes used).

3.5.1 **Maturity of Project Management and Adherence to Formal Procedures**

Organizations in which project management is more mature ("integrated" or "mature") and those that have and adhere to formal procedures are more likely to agree with the statements in Table 3-9 about process success, with the exception of "my competency as a project manager has increased" (which would be expected, as this statement pertains to the individual and not to the organization). The strength of agreement with these statements increases as the maturity increases or similarly as the adherence to procedures is stronger (using four categories for each scale, significant at 95% using the Jonckheere-Terpstra test).

Quality of Processes	Tend to Agree or Strongly Agree, %	
	(A)	**(B)**
Lessons are generalizable to other projects (11b)	76.8	63.9
Outputs are truthful (11d)	76.4	59.7
We identify clear issues (10a)	81.8	53.8
We prioritize issues (10b)	69.6	48.9
We learn complex lessons (11a)	66.5	49.8
We avoid blame (10c)	64.2	48.9
People share learning about failures (10d)	68.4	45.9
We create knowledge rather than simply collecting data (11c)	54.3	36.5
We get to the root causes of project outcomes (10e)	54.1	27.1
Results of Lessons Learned	**Tend to Agree or Strongly Agree, %**	
	(A)	**(B)**
My competency as a project manager has increased (12c)	87.2	86.8
Project competency within the organization has increased (12b)	67.7	55.1
Projects are more successful (12a)	60.8	49.3
Transfer of Lessons Learned	**Tend to Agree or Strongly Agree, %**	
	(A)	**(B)**
Lessons learned move from the individual to the project team (16a)	62.3	33.5
Lessons learned are applied by other project teams (16c)	46.9	24.5
Learning is achieved across cultures (16d)	31.0	13.3
Lessons learned move from the project team to the organization (16b)	33.5	10.4

(A)=Companies that have and adhere to formal procedures
(B)=Companies that do not have or do not adhere to formal procedures

Table 3-9 **Companies that Have and Adhere to Formal Procedures Are More Likely to Agree with Success Statements with the Exception of "My Competency as a Project Manager Has Increased"**

To illustrate this point, the results for formal procedures are summarized in Table 3-9 (combined into two categories). The (similar) results for maturity are summarized in Appendix 3. The differences are particularly big for "we get to the root causes of project outcomes" and those statements concerning the transfer of lessons. For "lessons move from the project team to the organization," companies are more than three times more likely to agree if they have formal procedures (shown in Table 3-9) or their project management is integrated or mature (see Appendix 3).

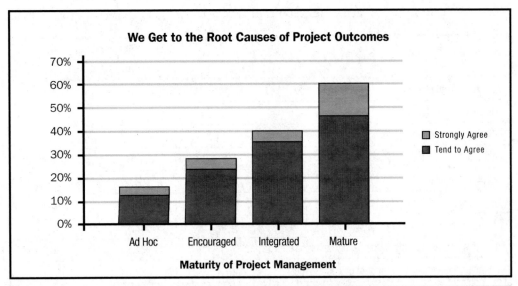

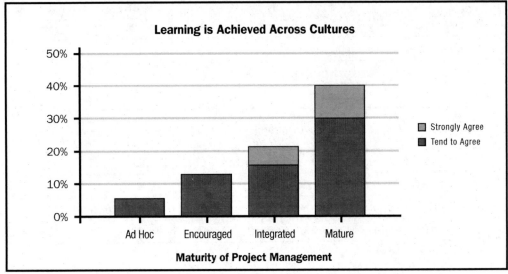

Figure 3-6 **Companies Where PM Is Mature Are Much More Likely to Agree with the Above Statements**

Similar results are shown in Appendix 3, showing the relationship between perceived success and the project-management maturity of the organization. Figure 3-6 illustrates two striking differences: the perception that "we get to the root causes of project outcomes" and the perception that "learning is achieved across cultures."

Organizations in which project management is less mature gain no significant benefit from having and adhering to formal procedures. There is a significant benefit to organizations when project management is integrated.

3.5.2 **Effectiveness of Doing Lessons Learned Throughout the Project**

Organizations that do lessons learned activities on a regular basis (on completion of major milestones or deliverables or at regular intervals) are more likely to agree with almost all of the above success statements (though, interestingly, not "we avoid issues of blame," "we learn complex lessons," "lessons are generalizable," "learning is achieved across cultures," and the individual statement "my own competency has increased"). This is true for many of the statements even after allowing for the maturity of the organization, as shown in Table 3-10.

We Get to the Root Causes of Project Outcomes	Tend to Agree or Strongly Agree, %	
	(A)	(B)
Mature (115)*	74.4	53.9
Integrated (193)*	61.0	34.9
Encouraged or ad hoc (147)	26.7	25.8
All responses (461, includes 6 for which maturity is not known)*	61.5	35.1
We Create Knowledge Rather than Simply Collecting Data	**Tend to Agree or Strongly Agree, %**	
	(A)	(B)
Mature (114)*	84.6	53.3
Integrated (193)	53.8	39.0
Encouraged or ad hoc (146)	26.7	34.4
All responses (460, includes 7 for which maturity is not known)*	62.1	40.3

* Indicates the difference is significant.
(A)=Organizations which do regular lessons learned.
(B)=Organizations which do not conduct regular lessons learned.

Table 3-10 **Organizations Are More Likely to Agree that Their Processes Are Successful if They Do Regular Lessons Learned**

3.5.3 **Other Demographics**

The perceived success of lessons learned processes was also compared with a number of other demographic indicators, in particular:

1. *Size of Projects*—There appears to be no relationship between the average size of projects and the success of lessons learned.

2. *Size of Organization*—The relationship between the size of the organization and the success of lessons learned appears to be U-shaped for several of the measures, with higher scores for the smallest organizations (under 100 employees) and lower for the middle category, that is, those with between 1,000 and 10,000 employees. This can be seen most clearly for statements assessing the transfer of lessons learned (see Figure 3-7). Differences are significant (smallest organizations higher than the mean, organizations in the middle category lower than the mean) for 16b (lessons learned move effectively beyond the project team to the organization) and 16c (lessons learned are applied by other project teams). For statements assessing the quality of the processes (Q10, 11), the U-shape is only significant for 11a (we learn complex lessons) for which organizations in the middle category have lower scores, and 11d (we achieve outputs that are truthful), for which smallest organizations have higher scores.

3. *A specific department for lessons learned*—Perhaps not surprisingly, organizations which have a specific department for lessons learned are significantly more likely to agree on all statements relating to the quality of the process, such as "we get to the root causes of project outcomes" and "we create knowledge rather than collecting data."

3.5.4 **Effectiveness of Different Processes**

It would also be useful to see which processes correspond to increased perceptions of success. The success criteria in Questions 10, 11, and 16 were compared within those organizations that did or did not use the processes listed in the questionnaire in Questions 7 and 8. The results are shown in Table 3-11, where an asterisk shows that a chi-squared test indicated that a process correlates with improved effectiveness. The first part of the table relates to processes for capturing lessons, the second part to processes for transferring lessons.

To capture lessons, the use of project audits and meetings correlate well; asking the customer and using an external facilitator do not correlate well. The relationships between meetings and successful processes all but disappear when controlling for project management maturity. The relationships between project audits disappear with the exception of one category: organizations where project management is "integrated." In

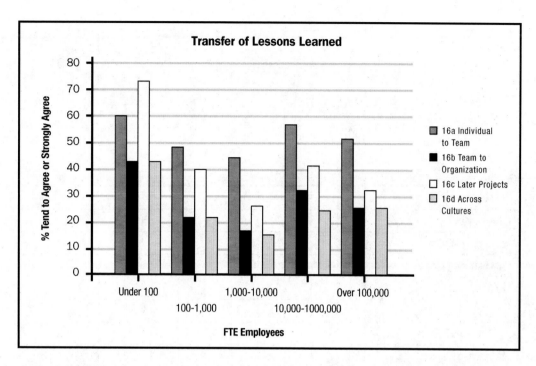

Figure 3-7 **Smaller Organizations Transfer Lessons More Effectively and Medium–Sized Less Effectively**

these organizations the relationship is significant for 10a, 10b and 10e, 11a, 11b and 11d, and 16a and 16b. (NB external team has been excluded from this analysis, as the number of cases was too small.)

Curiously, only 33.6% of organizations using project audits stated that they do lessons learned on a regular basis. The comparable figure for those not using project audits is 16.0%.

To transfer lessons, the use of almost any process appears to correlate with getting to the root causes of a problem and all aspects of transfer within the same culture. Many of these relationships disappear when controlling for project management maturity, although again where project management is "integrated," about half of the correlations persist. For organizations where project management is ad hoc or encouraged, there is a correlation between using presentations and transferring lessons to later projects. (Use of micro articles has been excluded, as the number of cases was too small.)

	10a Identify Clear Issues	10b Prioritize Issues	10c Avoid Blame	10d Share Failures	10e Get to Root Causes	11a Learn Complex Lessons	11b Lessons Generalizable	11c Create Knowledge	11d Outputs Truthful	16a Transfer Individual to Team	16b Transfer Team to Organization	16c Used for Later Projects	16d Across Cultures
7a Meetings	*	*		*	*					*	*		
7b Interviews	*			*							*		
7c Project Audits	*	*	*		*	*		*		*	*	*	*
7d Learning Diaries	*										*	*	
7e Narratives	*												
7f Ask Customer													
7g External Facilitator													
8a Training		*	*		*	*		*		*	*	*	*
8b Moving People			*										
8c IT Mediated	*	*	*		*	*		*		*	*	*	
8d Narratives		*	*	*	*					*	*	*	*
8e CoPs		*			*		*			*	*	*	*
8f Resources Center					*			*			*	*	
8g Mentoring		*	*	*	*	*	*	*	*	*	*	*	*
8h Presentations	*	*			*	*		*	*	*	*	*	
8j New Procedures				*	*			*	*	*	*	*	*
8k Documentation	*	*	*	*	*	*	*	*	*	*	*	*	*
8l Ad Hoc	*_ve	*_ve	*_ve	*_ve	*			*_ve	*_ve	*_ve	*_ve	*_ve	*_ve

*A chi-squared test indicated that these processes correlated with improved effectiveness.

Table 3-11 **The Perceived Effectiveness of Different Processes**

3.6 **What Do You Think Is Best Practice?**

This section discusses the results of Questions 19–22, aimed at finding out what respondents felt was best practice in the area.

3.6.1 **Best Practice for Learning Lessons (Q19, 20)**
The questionnaire presented the respondent with a set of practices and asked which did

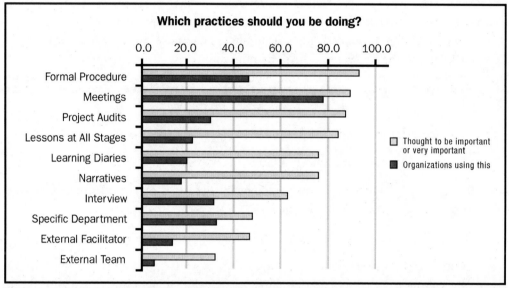

	Respondents Who Consider This Important or Very Important, %	Organizations Who Do This, %
Use a formal procedure	92.2	45.9
Meetings/workshops	88.7	77.8
Regular project audits	86.4	29.3
Collect lessons at all stages of the project	83.3	20.9
Learning diaries/logs	75.6	19.5
Narratives	75.0	17.1
Interviews	61.9	30.4
Specific department	46.8	31.7
External facilitator	45.9	12.6
External team	30.6	4.4

Figure 3-8 **The Disparity between Processes Project Managers Think Their Organizations Should Be Doing to Capture Lessons and Those Which Are Actually Done**

the respondent think their organization should be doing to learn lessons. All were felt to be important by a majority of the respondents, except for the use of a specific lessons learned department (the modal response was "useful but not essential"), and the use of external project facilitators or teams. However, there is a big discrepancy between the importance assigned by project managers to the various practices for learning lessons and their use in practice. The biggest disparities arise for collecting lessons at all stages of the project life cycle, learning diaries, narratives, and use of an external team. The results are shown in Figure 3-8.

Respondents were asked whether there were any other practices their organization should be following to learn lessons from projects. Of the 522 respondents, 159 gave answers (excluding those who responded "no"). A number of those were simply "do anything" or "actually carry out the processes." The remaining comments gave interesting insights into the feelings of the respondents, some of which were quite lengthy. A number of insights can be gained from the overall response:

- At least 20 of the answers asked for a searchable database tool.

- The theme of "communication" was a frequent response.

- Four responses looked for outsiders to be involved in the lessons learned gathering processes.

- Three responses looked for incentives for staff to be involved.

- A number of answers, rather than suggesting new processes, emphasized processes already quoted in the questionnaire; some made suggestions that hadn't been touched upon. Some particular techniques suggested include:

  - Retrospectives (two responses)

  - Root cause analysis (two responses)

  - External investigators

  - Case studies for use as teaching propositions during training

  - Responsibility matrices

  - Expert judges

  - Metrics collection

  - Strategic SWOT changes review

  - Exclude politics from lessons learned

  - Incorporating lessons learned in risk discussions

- Benchmarking with similar external project organizations
- Individual log book for recording daily activities
- Central project management office.

3.6.2 Best Practice for Transferring Lessons (Q21, 22)

The questionnaire presented the respondent with a set of practices and asked which practices their organization should be doing to transfer lessons to future projects. All of the practices were felt to be important by a majority of the respondents, except for the use of micro articles/video clips and the use of a specific lessons learned department (again, the modal response was "useful but not essential").

There were big disparities across all techniques between the importance assigned by project managers to the various practices for transferring lessons and their use in practice (the technique "people trained to retrieve lessons learned" had not been asked), as shown in Figure 3-9.

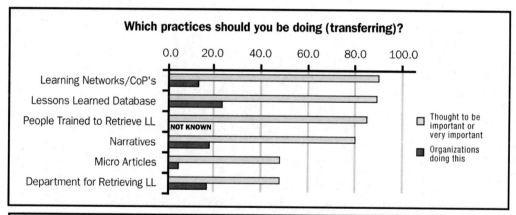

	Respondents Who Consider This Important or Very Important, %	Organizations Who Do This, %
Learning networks/communities of practice	88.9	11.6
Lessons learned database	87.0	22.0
People trained to retrieve lessons learned	84.0	not known
Narratives	78.5	17.1
Micro articles	46.1	3.0
Department for retrieving lessons learned	46.0	15.0

Figure 3-9 **The Disparity Between Processes Which Project Managers Think Their Organizations Should Be Doing to Transfer Lessons and Those Which Are Actually Done**

Respondents were again asked whether there were any ways in which access to lessons learned from previous projects could be made easier. Answers were received from 128 respondents (excluding those that said "no" or something similar), although some of the remainder just made general comments. Approximately one-half of the answers either stated that a database or similar system was needed or assumed its existence in their answer:

- At least 61 answers talked about a database (with some answers emphasizing the categorization capabilities).

- A more sophisticated document management or content management or other web-based systems were mentioned in 11 answers. A few respondents mentioned proprietary names (including a leader in integrated enterprise content management solutions).

- At least 12 answers were specifically geared towards socialization ideas, generating transfer through interpersonal relationships within the community.

- Another 10 answers related to embedding lessons learned within company procedures and processes.

- A few answers gave innovative ideas, such as audio-narratives; "townhall" meetings or micro articles (published passively on a website and actively in company news); and running fake projects to build personal experience of change.

Two responses are worth reproducing in full, as they explain the "lived experience" that is important for absorbing lessons:

> "No one gains experience through reading cold data. The only way to gain experience is to do something yourself or empathize with someone who has. This is important in organizational learning as it hangs a lesson in a story that someone remembers and puts into their own context— aka religious texts, fables, legends, history etc."

> "I don't believe a third party can be responsible. They didn't live the "issues." I believe it is the project team itself that must be responsible for gathering and documenting the lessons learned. If a third party then is responsible for communicating and facilitating knowledge transfer, then that would be useful."

3.6.3 What Stops People from Doing More? (Q23)

Respondents were asked what hindered people in their organizations from putting more effort into the lessons learned process (both capture and transfer). Only 8.4% of people agreed that they already put in enough effort. The main reasons for not doing more are lack of employee time (67%) and lack of management support. The top five reasons, cited by more than 50% of the respondents, are shown in Table 3-12.

Reason	Responses %
Lack of employee time	67.0
Lack of management support	62.5
Lack of incentive	53.7
Lack of resources	53.1
Lack of clear guidelines	52.3
Lack of support from others in organization	32.2
Our processes don't capture useful lessons	21.9
Data repository too hard to search	20.9
Lessons are not transferable	13.3
Wrong people are involved	8.8
We already put in enough effort	8.4

Table 3-12 **The Main Reasons for Not Putting More Effort into the Lessons Learned Process**

When asked if there were any "other" reasons, only 63 replies were given, which can be divided equally in the following four groups:

* Culture; many of these respondents specifically mentioned a "blame culture"

* Lack of a database

* Lack of incentive for a process consuming too much time or effort

* Other responses.

3.6.4 Narratives

Finally (following the interest in narratives found in the literature survey that prefaced this work), respondents were asked whether they felt that more "stories" or case studies would be of significant value, to which 83% responded "yes."

3.7 Conclusions

Some conclusions taken from this chapter are summarized below.

* There is a big disparity between the processes that project managers think their organizations should be doing and those that are actually done. About 62% of project management mature organizations in the survey carry out lessons learned activities after all or most projects. This correlates to 41% where project management is integrated and only 14% where project management is encouraged or ad hoc. Specific departments were responsible for lessons learned in 32% of the organizations. Outside personnel (customers or subcontractors) are often involved in lessons learned; however, internal staff other than project management, senior management, or technical staff were rarely present.

* The least successful aspect of learning is the transfer of lessons learned within an organization, particularly the transfer of lessons from the project team to the organization. There are also key problems with getting to the root causes of project outcomes and creating knowledge rather than collecting data.

* Organizations where project management is mature are four times more likely to do lessons learned after all or most projects than organizations where it is not mature. When lessons learned are done, those organizations are three times as likely to do it at regular intervals throughout the project and are much less likely to do it only in response to a problem or business need. Organizations where project management is less mature gain little benefit from having and adhering to formal procedures, but there is a significant benefit where project management is integrated.

* A number of factors correlate with more effective learning, including maturity of project management, use of formal procedures, having a specific department, doing lessons learned throughout the project, and doing project audits. These relationships are most notable in areas where organizations experience the greatest difficulties (transfer, getting to the root causes, and creating knowledge).

* Organizations in which project management is more mature and those which have and adhere to formal procedures are much more likely to believe that their lessons learned procedures are successful in achieving their aims.

* There is no single process that improves the effectiveness of lessons learned for those organizations where project management is least mature. Several processes appear to improve significantly the effectiveness when project management is integrated and a few when project management is mature.

- Lack of employee time and lack of management support are the leading reasons for lessons learned not being undertaken; other reasons were lack of incentive/ resources/guidelines and the idea of a blame culture.

Some additional particular points:
- The most successful aspect is the increased competency of individual project managers. This does not seem to depend on how the organization does lessons learned.

- Smaller organizations appear to be more successful at transferring lessons learned, and organizations with 1,000 to 10,000 employees less successful.

- About 20% of organizations benchmark or measure their processes for effectiveness.

- Only 8% of project managers think that they put enough effort into doing lessons learned. Lack of time and lack of management support are the main reasons given for not doing more.

4

INTERVIEWS: DO ORGANIZATIONS LEARN FROM PROJECTS?

4.1 Introduction

This chapter describes the results of some interviews with managers on the use of lessons learned from projects within their organizations. The interviews followed, and were informed by, the Zoomerang™ survey of how project managers learn lessons from projects, and whether they believe it to be successful. Six senior and project management personnel were interviewed, using semi-structured interviews in order to establish processes, seek views about these practices, and investigate any anecdotes that might indicate success or failure of the practices. Five of the interviews were with UK managers and one with a North American manager; all but one were by telephone, as dictated by the financial constraints of the project.

The three main studies are with companies that successfully carry out lessons learned activities. However, being quite different types of companies, their solutions are very different. One carries out fairly small projects; one carries out very large, complex projects; the third is a public body carrying out mainly IT projects. These can be summarized as follows. The first three case studies then follow, in a common format.

Organization C—This is an example of a company carrying out small-scale projects, which are fairly self-contained in a small unit. It has a well-enforced but fairly informal lessons learned process. Lessons are gathered by discussion then presented at a meeting. The output included elements such as lessons, tips, or process improvements. These lessons were "pushed" out, then available on a website for proactive retrieval. The company clearly felt this process was successful. This type of process appeared to be appropriate for this type and size of project and organization. Narratives, not surprisingly, were not felt to be helpful.

Organization G—This case study is an example of a very large company performing very large, complex projects. Formal procedures are eschewed in favor of an approach closer to communities of practice. For these complex projects, socialization is perhaps a more appropriate approach than databases and IT-mediated approaches. The projects are long, so "lessons learned" only at the end of a project or even at phase-gate makes less sense—lessons learned needs to be a continuous process. Narratives might help but there was a perceived difficulty in the time investment required. One problem throughout the lessons learned system for this study was getting people to contribute.

Organization P—This is an example of a huge UK government organization—the UK government favoring PRINCE2-type approaches (Office of Government Commerce [2002]). The system that was developed fits within the organizational stage-gate system and uses a data-base approach, with a central Centre of Excellence acting as custodians. This approach is distinguished from simple database approaches, particularly in having strong elements of narrative to bring the lessons alive, which was felt to have significantly added to the success of the system, as well as some proactive dissemination channels.

4.2 Organization C

4.2.1 The Organization and Interviewee

Company C is a UK-based element of a U.S. technology company whose sales are in the multi-billion dollar category annually. Projects within Company C can take from approximately three months up to two years; project teams tend to be fairly small (under 100 people). Company C has a PMO; this was set up essentially because a number of project managers (including the interviewee) wanted to "preach the [project-management] word." The responsibility of the PMO is to improve projects, improve developmental skills of project managers, institutionalize the best practice, and improve the tools and systems. The interviewee is a program manager within the PMO, who is a PMP.

4.2.2 Background to the Lessons Learned Process

Over a decade ago, the parent company introduced a stage-gate project system, which included a lessons learned process (written by someone external to the company), although it is not clear that the procedure was followed other than nominally. Around five years ago CMM was introduced into the company and later CMMI; these both updated the earlier lessons learned procedure and considerably reduced its length. The PMO has control of the lessons learned procedure.

4.2.3 What Is the Procedure for Capturing Lessons?

The project procedure has about 20 milestones, the last of which is "lessons learned." A lessons learned activity ought to be carried out for 100% of projects, although it is probably performed for around 80% of projects (the reasons for it not being carried out usually are either because the project manager has gone to another project or because projects drag on without a clear end-point and with many clean-up activities). The PMO is also starting to encourage lessons learned activities at mid-project. The procedure is essentially as follows:

- The PMO organizes a monthly meeting and identifies projects that have reached this milestone. The PMO will contact the project manager (PM) and ask whether the PM is ready to present the lessons learned.

- Generally the PM puts together the lessons, but the PMO will help if it is the first time for the project manager or the project is "politically sensitive."

- The project manager will send out an e-mail asking "what went wrong or right and why," gather the information, and meet with a core group if feasible to review the information gathered.

- There is a template for reporting the lessons learned, consisting of an overview, the people involved, what went well, what went badly, and recommendations and project metrics.

- The PMO will put out the agenda for the meeting in which approximately three projects will be reported (the metrics are recorded but not presented).

Lessons are recorded during the project by means of the Project Control Document (an Excel document), which has a "lessons learned tab," where notes can be recorded to help the memory; this is revisited on at least a monthly basis; while this perhaps does not go into much depth it does help recall.

4.2.4 What Is the Procedure for Disseminating Lessons?

At each monthly meeting, there is a presentation of lessons learned. The audience at this meeting generally is composed of a dozen to two dozen people, consisting of project managers and the managers one level more senior, but this represents perhaps one-quarter to one-third of the available population of such people. The PMO chairs the meeting and captures the action items, etc., which, for each meeting, will usually consist of approximately two actions, one recommendation for a process update, and six "top tips" (in the format "If you are faced by <describe issue or situation>, then you should consider <describe recommendation>"). The PMO then disseminates these and puts the presentation on the internet.

If project managers wish to proactively retrieve the lessons:

- The lessons are on the website, split into a few types of projects. At the time of the interview, there were perhaps ten projects per year for each type over a three-year period; the manager would pick some of these and read them.

- There is also an Excel spreadsheet with all the "top tips" in it, which consisted of 100 at the time of this study.

4.2.5 **How Successful Is the process?**

The interviewee was asked about "success" in a number of ways:

- *What is the value in the system?* Some lessons have clearly been learned—some "top tips" that existed one-and-a-half to two years ago have now disappeared. It was felt that knowledge sharing generally is good and that the system identified gaps in the organization (e.g., "logistics aren't working") and/or processes. The interviewee considered both sharing knowledge and identifying process/organization gaps as important, perhaps equally important.

- *How is the process measured?* The measure taken is the average number of days after project completion to the completion of the lessons learned process (aiming for less than 30 days); however, there is no tangible measure of "value." There are some intangible measures, such as the problems ("points of pain") disappearing since a couple of years ago. However, measuring improvements in project management is important and comes as part of CMMI—this is part of their active governance and feeds into their estimation process.

- *What blockages are perceived in the process?* The interviewee did not see any major blockages and indicated that processes do change if necessary.

- *Does the process get to the root causes of problems?* The interviewee felt that the process did find the root causes. The e-mail that is circulated (to everyone involved in the project) asks about root causes.

- *How does lessons learned feed into the organization's processes?* Senior management attends the presentations. Approximately one item per meeting is a recommendation to senior management (e.g., "purchasing consistently causes a roadblock in area X . . ."). Also, the head of the PMO goes to the weekly senior managers' meeting and provides input into the strategy.

- *How could the process be made better?* The interviewee would have liked more people to attend the presentations but commented that perhaps one-fourth to one-third of the population is all that can be expected (some say they're too busy, some feel it is not their learning style; generally the same people attend meetings).

The interviewee, when asked whether narratives would help, felt that it was the top tips that people related to, not the stories.

4.3 **Organization G**

4.3.1 **The Organization and Interviewee**

Organization G is a UK-based engineering company with annual sales of approximately $10 billion (U.S.). The company performs many types of projects. Looking at their three main sectors, programs in one would typically last three to five years and of the order of $100 million (U.S.) or higher per year; in the second sector, programs would last typically 20 years; and in the third, a project would run typically around six months long and with a value of $5 million (U.S.).

The interviewee is the director of a Central Programme Management Centre, which has a role within the company to improve project and program management, which includes auditing projects. The role is encouraging, but the advice is not enforceable. (Although if a project goes wrong, then a justification as to why the advice wasn't followed needs to be provided.)

4.3.2 **Background to the Lessons Learned Process**

The organization does not have formal project management lessons learned procedures. There are detailed procedures for sharing lessons learned and full-time personnel responsible for this, but these are engineering lessons learned. For project management lessons, there are high-level project management principles, which include lessons learned, but there is no detailed guidance on how to carry this out—the process relies on the goodwill of project managers.

4.3.3 **What Is the Procedure for Capturing Lessons?**

The procedures are currently in transition. When the high-level company project management principles were originally prepared, the intention was that lessons learned would be performed at the end of the project. However, the interviewee felt that, by that point, the important people would have been removed from a project (the people remaining may not be the most appropriate to write up the project). Thus, the interviewee was much more in favor of lessons learned being a *continual* process throughout the duration of the project, particularly since lessons are learned in real-time. The interviewee encourages networks of like-minded people who meet, which are essentially communities of practice.

4.3.4 **What Is the Procedure for Disseminating Lessons?**

The department circulates lessons learned if they've come to the department's notice; they have identified some 200–300 people in the project management community. There is no permanent record of the lessons, because the lessons go stale too quickly.

In the project start-up process, the project team "fans out" across the company, to gain advice before they start. Note that this "fanning out" includes an "extended family" beyond the company (e.g., to the project-management community, and there is a system whereby customers, suppliers, and/or partners get asked also).

4.3.5 How Successful Is the Process?

The interviewee was asked about "success" in a number of ways:

- *Are the procedures believed to be successful?* A recent major project had just followed the above procedure, and this was "the best set-up project recently." Because of the casual networking, the team went to the right people and got the right advice. They did have repeated mistakes in the past—he believes this real-time system will lessen this.

- *Is the process measured/benchmarked?* There is no measuring or benchmarking, as there was felt to be no objective way to do this. Subjectively, one can feel the difference in a project—the amount of assurance, confidence, and a feeling that the team is acting in a systemic way rather than "running around with fire buckets."

- *What blockages are perceived?* The main problem appeared to be how busy potential contributors were. The interviewee would like to bring some sort of system into this process, but people don't have the time for this.

- *Does the process get to the root causes of problems?* The interviewee felt that this process possibly does not get to the root causes. The engineering system (where lessons learned are offered up and a "committee of wise men" review them) possibly does, but not for project management.

The interviewee was also asked whether narratives would help; it was felt that they would; however, the difficulty is getting people to write them up, which is a really big investment of time.

4.4 Organization P

4.4.1 The Organization and Interviewee

Organization P is a major government department in the UK with an annual budget in excess of $10 billion U.S. The "program, systems and delivery" is a central service working across all areas. Within this group is the Directorate for Project Management, which does not manage projects hands-on but provides standards, guidance, and help to PMOs. Projects for which the directorate is involved cover a wide variety, particularly including IT but also business change, and of all sizes: a recent major project was multi-agency and worth well over $1 billion U.S. The program, systems, and delivery group is responsible for supporting learning from projects. The interviewee is a senior member of that directorate.

4.4.2 **Background to the Lessons Learned Process**

The department had a standard program/project life cycle, and a formal lessons learned procedure within that, which the current department inherited. However, during a recent reorganization, the department was concerned that project learning wasn't happening; previously, lessons were transferred by individuals, and frequently lessons simply disappeared from the organization. The process was therefore revised as part of an overall drive to improve project quality standards, and the new process was launched around five months before this interview. While lessons learned activities previously were carried out only at the end of a project (even if it was the result of a one-year duration and the project team had moved on), now lessons learned is carried out for all projects (mandated by stage-gate system) and in-project learning is checked at stage-ends as well as project-ends.

It should be noted that the system is moving soon to a different group within the department; but the interviewee noted that senior management was strongly supportive, even to the very top level of the department.

4.4.3 **What Is the Procedure for Capturing Lessons?**

Within projects, any member of the project team can identify learning opportunities during the project. Lessons learned should be on the agenda for the main meetings (e.g., biweekly or monthly "checkpoint" meetings, or at risk review/issue management meetings). These get documented onto a lessons learned form, which rather than just being a piece of advice captures the story, including:

- description of the situation that led to the lesson

- impact of the situation

- alternatives considered

- actions taken

- results achieved

- shared learning, that is, concisely presented transferable advice.

Lessons learned are categorized. Each lessons learned goes to the PMO, who logs it and looks at the quality; the PMO ensures that the lesson is learned within the project and considers whether the lesson could be applicable elsewhere in the department. If the project is applicable, the PMO asks the project manager to allow it to be shared wider; if that is agreed, then it goes on to a national searchable lessons learned database (having been re-checked and validated in the Centre of Excellence).

There is a formal requirement at the end of each stage to show that the project has paid proper attention to lessons learned; the work performed is required to be included in the stage-gate review document to ensure that the information is captured. There is also a small team reviewing all lessons in the database, to determine whether procedures/processes/standards/training, etc., need to be changed to gain this learning, that is, to look for improvement opportunities.

4.4.4 **What Is the procedure for disseminating lessons?**

Dissemination of lessons is done by means of a website, access to the national lessons learned database, and strategic general learning; also some proactive dissemination is carried out by the directorate.

Each project has a start-up meeting at the beginning of each phase with the Centre of Excellence, and lessons learned is on the agenda for this meeting.

4.4.5 **How Successful Is the Process?**

The interviewee was asked about success in a number of ways:

- *Are the procedures felt to be successful?* The procedures are felt to be much more successful than those used previously, due to the active in-time capture and ensuring quality lessons rather than vacuous ones; to some extent, quality is built in to lessons learned because they are required to be written up.

- *What is the value in the system?* The directorate is starting to see value, for example in filling gaps in the project life cycle. The directorate believes that the process is generally successful because they do not expect to see the same lessons repeated, due to the application of lessons in future processes.

- *Is the process measured or benchmarked?* The interviewee felt that value can't be quantified, so essentially there is no measurement of effectiveness or benchmarking. The department only occasionally tried quantification in the past (e.g., statements such as "we did X and saved N weeks"). The directorate is collecting anecdotal evidence by collecting and disseminating lessons and on lessons being used, and it is planning a study after 12 months of the new process to look at effectiveness (e.g., measures of awareness of the process, adherence to the process, number and quality of lessons being recorded).

- *What blockages are currently perceived?* This is a new process so it is too early to identify definite blockages, but the interviewee could envision five potential blockages:

  1. If in the past there was only lip-service paid to lessons learned, there would now need to be a culture change that might take two years;

  2. Some lessons are not released by the project manager because they are not anonymous;

3. The project manager can also be a blockage;

4. It is important that the Centre of Excellence looks for and actively markets lessons. Otherwise, they will not be disseminated;

5. In view of the impending move of the responsibility of the system, the interviewee had concern that if not properly resourced, then improvement opportunities might not be captured.

- *Does the process get to the root causes of problems?* The interviewee believed that the process was beginning to get to root causes and noted that the database contained a mixture of lessons learned in-project and post-project, generally with the input for in-project lessons from meetings, so more than one person has developed them.

The interviewee was also asked whether narratives help. The interviewee agreed that they do, as described previously. The reader needs to see where the advice comes from, that is, the type of project and what impact the actions had (in other words, why one should follow the advice) in order to see the real situation; and readers can follow up the lesson with the actual project manager. The interviewee felt that the change of capturing entire stories was one of the most important changes made.

4.5 **Additional Case Studies**

In order to gain more insight, three other case studies were carried out. One was from a consultant who provided lessons learned services, one from a company similar to one previously discussed but with an interviewee external to project management, and the third from an interviewee who had set up a system and subsequently parted from the organization. These case studies are summarized in this section, and the case study descriptions are presented in Sections 4.6 through 4.7, in a similar format but somewhat briefer than the format used previously.

- *Organization W* is a consultancy carrying out lessons learned workshops for major companies. The lessons-capture techniques, which were centered around a workshop but captured the background and stories as well as lessons, appeared to work well. There were clear issues in disseminating the lessons and a need to embed the capture-system within a learning process.

- *Organization L* is a very large company similar to Organization G, where the culture was changing to be more project management oriented. The lessons learned process here focused on bids. Because all bids were prepared in one geographical location, gathering previous lessons could be done through socialization. During projects, which might be carried out in teams distributed worldwide, lessons learned is embedded within a formal risks and opportunities process. Again, there are possibly some issues of dissemination.

- *Organization S* is a large company with a carefully planned lessons learned process, which is described. The write-up particularly shows some of the inter-personal issues that need to be considered in planning such a process. It also illustrates the relationship between the "stories" of a project and its documentation.

4.6 Organization W

4.6.1 The Organization and Interviewee

Organization W is a global consultancy based in the UK, with turnover of the order of $50 million U.S. The organization as a whole deals mainly with construction, typically seeing interventions into projects rather than whole projects, typically working in projects of around $100 million U.S. The group to which the interviewee is a senior member deals with rail 50% of the time. The interviewee mainly discussed his involvement with two very large rail organizations (X and Z described in 4.6.2 and 4.6.3), although a few of the projects are related to the UK health sector (Y). The interviewee noted that the consultancy's experience of industry is non-typical, in that they are more likely to be called if a lessons learned exercise is needed, so they typically do not work with organizations that don't do lessons learned.

4.6.2 Background to the Lessons Learned Process

There are no formal guidelines within the organization, but rather it works within the systems of the client organization. There were formal methods for all three of the organizations (X, Y, and Z). X and Z have program management teams that monitor key performance indicators (KPIs) of projects. These two organizations either carry out lessons learned themselves or use consultants to carry out a workshop. The interviewee felt that X and Z were good at performing this because they are process driven in that they have a well-defined project management process, and one of the project start-up activities includes reviewing lessons learned from previous projects (although he had no knowledge as to whether this was done properly). Y does carry out lessons learned but generally uses consultants. (The interviewee felt this was in contrast to construction, where lessons learned are very rare.)

4.6.3 What Is the Procedure for Capturing Lessons?

The interviewee's standard process is to hold a fairly free workshop, covering the project team, contractors, operations staff (that is, those using the system being developed), and sometimes the client (depending on the outcome of the project). Lessons are then added to the library (at the time, they were being converted to a database). The meeting lasts one day (for a typical, say, $20 million U.S. job).

Z's process, in particular, was to hold a workshop, with pre-specified keywords, which were added to the library of lessons learned reports (the organization was in the process of developing a searchable database, but it was not finished at that time).

In these examples, lessons learned was only done at the end of the project (except for some technical issues). The interviewee recognized the issue that many members of the project team change as you go through the project (except for some senior managers); however, those key people that are still in the organization get invited back to the workshop; but the process still depends on the participants' memory.

4.6.4 What Is the Procedure for Disseminating Lessons?

The organization doesn't get involved in the dissemination within the client companies, but the interviewee did feel that lessons weren't proactively pushed; in other words, people were expected to look them up.

4.6.5 How Successful Is the process?

The interviewee was asked about "success" in a number of ways:

- *What is the value in the system?* The interviewee believed the lessons to be useful (although see notes on blockages below).

- *Is the process measured or benchmarked?* There was no measurement, and the interviewee was not sure how this could be done (although noted that using outside consultants somewhat serves as a benchmark).

- *What is good in the system?* The interviewee considered that a good element was the facilitated workshop where there are all the stakeholders participating and all contributing—and particularly because the workshop is explicitly non-blame.

- *What blockages are perceived?*

  1. The interviewee believed the main blockage to be in dissemination because sometimes the data is not completed, and it is often not high enough on a manager's priority list. Senior management does not necessarily strongly encourage use of the system.

  2. It takes an effort to proactively look up lessons. (The interviewee suggested that if there was a database and a way of linking the database to the project initiation process, then this process would flow well.)

  3. The interviewee felt there was also a bureaucratic mentality in some parts of the organization that was reluctant to change.

4. Lessons learned do not affect the organization's strategy. Theoretically, lessons to change a process should go to the QA organization, and if it detects a trend (for example, if this lesson happens frequently), they would look at changing the process. However, in the interviewee's experience this doesn't happen, but there were instances where it should have; there were some repeated mistakes, so that prior to working on a typical project(s), "6 out of the top 10 lessons" were predictable.

- *Does the process get to the root causes of problems?* The clients believe that the process gets to root causes, by looking at positive and negative lessons, and for those important points that spark debate and cause one to look carefully at the entire process. Having said that, the interviewee acknowledged that this observation was based on a workshop of only one day (although on a project that the consultants already know well—the process would need to be much longer if the consultants were coming in "cold"). There is a need to balance costs and benefits from the process.

The interviewee was also asked whether narratives help. A typical report in this system would have many pages of text, which would include stories of what happened and what people said. An extensive report like this would allow a future project manager to review the background and the sequence of events, which is considered to be valuable.

4.7 Organization L

4.7.1 The Organization and Interviewee

Organization L is a company that is made up of approximately one half of a North American engineering group whose revenues are over $10 billion per year. The interviewee is responsible for marketing and product planning for the company, and thus also provides input to strategic planning. The interviewee is therefore not in a project management function and is providing an outside view. Projects in this part of the company range from small (around $50 million) to very large (getting into the billions). Although the company has tens of thousands of employees worldwide, and projects can involve teams distributed worldwide, all bids are prepared essentially in the same building.

4.7.2 Background to the Lessons Learned Process

The role of project management and its procedure has changed, and was changing, within the company. The role of project management had been significantly enhanced within the company, so that project managers are in charge of a project right from the bid stage, with ultimate responsibility for a project lying with the project manager. This was a significant change to the culture and organization from previous years. There is no specific department or unit responsible for supporting learning, but the project director who is responsible for the bid performs the lessons learned and initiates the start-up meeting if successful.

4.7.3 What Is the Procedure for Capturing Lessons?

- During bid preparation, the project manager gathers the bid team and does an activity on lessons learned from previous projects. Initially, these lessons were based on recall but were becoming a more formalized process whereby the lessons learned are documented.

- A lessons learned activity is conducted after each bid.

- During the contract period, the contract is reviewed every month, risks and opportunities are analyzed throughout, and the lessons learned are obtained from these monthly reports.

- There is no central repository of lessons.

4.7.4 What Is the Procedure for Disseminating Lessons?

- The primary time to look at the lessons learned is at the start of a new project.

- All bids are prepared essentially in the same building, so when lessons are required, all of the people who have the lessons in their heads are on the premises, as is access to the post-bid lessons learned documents. (They are also aware of other people in other divisions who might be helpful.)

- The post-bid lessons learned can also feed into strategy planning.

- For major lessons learned (e.g., major important bids that are lost), lessons learned will be reviewed by the management committee for senior management.

- Every month the president of the group holds a monthly operations review of risks and opportunities. This helps to share lessons globally among the divisions of the organization.

4.7.5 How Successful Is the Process?

The interviewee was asked about "success" in a number of ways:

- *Are the procedures successful?* It was not clear or perhaps it was too early for the interviewee to form a view. The interviewee did have some sense of repeated mistakes.

- *What is the value in the system? Is the process measured/benchmarked?* It is clear that some procedures or processes were being changed because of lessons learned.

The company has not yet carried out any evaluation, let alone any continual refinement.

- *What blockages are perceived?* Dissemination was felt to be part of the problem. The interviewee felt that the system was more oriented towards senior management learning lessons and not sharing them throughout the company.

- *Does the process get to the root causes of problems?* These lessons learned activities are carried out for bids, so there isn't the same need to look for root causes. During projects, root causes are much easier to determine because of the constant risk and opportunity review process. It was clear that the company saw the need to find root causes and set a goal to include this in their process.

The interviewee was also asked whether narratives help. It was felt that the use of narratives comes about naturally as the system is being built by the same people who are recording lessons learned.

4.8 Organization S

4.8.1 The Organization and Interviewee

The interviewee had recently left a position within a major UK-based information organization with an annual turnover of approximately $5 billion (U.S.) Within that position he was responsible (amongst others) for lessons learned. The interview focused on the system(s) built there, although there had recently been a company reorganization de-emphasizing the project management approach, focusing more on business processes than on project management, with Centres of Excellence moved into vertical lines within the company. All of the projects discussed for Organization S are IT projects. Large initiative projects could span four years and many millions of dollars and could involve a worldwide initiative; "small" might mean projects taking six months, in a single center using approximately 40 people.

4.8.2 Background to the Lessons Learned Process

There was a master Project Management Office (PMO) for the corporation and satellite lower-level PMOs throughout the world. The interviewee was responsible for lessons learned.

Lessons learned were only performed at the end of the project; however, mid-project reviews were also performed. As the company went through a number of changes, it was decided not to perform multidisciplinary reviews at stage-gates in order to avoid conflict.

4.8.3 **What Is the Procedure for Capturing Lessons?**

Every large initiative was mandated to have a paper debrief, using a template, with probing questions. The answers were recorded as the initiative progressed. No recommendations or interpretations were made at this point, and this paper debrief was published (there were often embarrassing comments sometimes about senior management). The interviewee analyzed these, and, upon agreement, the debrief was then put on a project register as a final document.

4.8.4 **What Is the Procedure for Disseminating Lessons?**

A piece of software (based on Planview) was used as a knowledge center, giving information for a project manager, with color-coding/dashboards, etc., and a pyramid structure to enable drilling down. A project manager's assistant would be shown the system by the PMO.

4.8.5 **How Successful Is the Process?**

The interviewee was asked about "success" in a number of ways:

- *Are the procedures successful?* The project process did change due to the lessons learned process. The interviewee proposed a system to review the project process, but that did not happen before the reorganization. It should be noted that the debrief reveals the successes as well as the problems.

- *What blockages are perceived?* Many issues were due to people who did not necessarily change their attitudes. Examples of problems were confrontational meetings, people thinking about the next stage of career or job once a project was finished, and people busy with other things. Also, the discipline of this process is difficult unless a company is stable, therefore this depends on the company itself.

Does the process get to the root causes of problems? The interviewee felt that it did.

The interviewee was also asked whether narratives help. In this system, the briefing of the project was published in a story version, with a link to the full debrief, for general consumption. The interviewee considered that this sort of version was needed but felt that there was also the need for solid documentation as these served two different purposes.

5
CASE STUDY IN PRACTICE

5.1 Background

Activity 4 of this work looked at a specific project within one organization to see how lessons are gathered and to see how they can be disseminated. The organization studied was a small UK governmental body, which followed the standard process within the UK public sector, PRINCE2 (Office of Government Commerce [2002]), in which end-of-project reports were prepared, including lessons learned. The organization had recently set up a Centre of Excellence for managing change, which had collated lessons into a small but growing lessons learned database; however, the content of this database was felt to be somewhat anodyne and it was suggested that full value was not being obtained from the lessons learned process. The author of this report therefore undertook to look briefly into whether more value could be obtained from the lessons learned process.

The organization had recently undertaken a significant change program surrounding an IT implementation with significant implications to the manner in which the organization operated. Project managers were brought in from an outside contractor. The program had overruns in time and cost (although not drastically), but had delivered the deliverables that were required. Lessons learned activities had been carried out both for the program and for constituent projects. It was decided to use the two main constituents of this program as an example, to see whether more value could be gained from the lessons of these projects. The resulting report, which was some 6,000 words, was not therefore a review of the program, but rather the program was used as a vehicle for studying the lessons learned process and making proposals for improvement.

5.2 Interviews of Project Participants

Semi-structured interviews were held with a number of project participants, and using issues that had been raised in the reports asked two questions: "why" and "so what?" (note that "what" came later in the causal process). Questions were also asked about the lessons learned process itself.

The first type of question looked at issues raised in the program report and the overall lateness and overspending, and asked why these occurred. Working back along the causal chain appeared to give some potentially useful lessons, although there was insufficient time to explore this in-depth in this study, and some fundamental reasons for the project issues were identified. The survey of practice in Section 2.3 found that only 40% of the participants felt they got to the root causes of project outcomes, and organizations identified problems with getting to root causes as important, and this was something that could perhaps be developed further in the organization.

The second type of question ("so what?") explored the effects of identified project issues. This was necessary to understand why these issues are important. The lessons learned database as it currently existed was normative, stating what "should" be done. One problem with this is that, while these might be generally correct statements, it might not be apparent why they are being made (and, being generalizations, there might be exceptions). For example, a statement that "high-level commitment is important" is clearly correct; but the statement that "lack of high-level commitment has been found to lead to resources not being available so is disrupting to projects" would have given some reason for a project manager to take notice. It was felt that this might be contributing to the feeling that the current database seems anodyne.

The program studied, although large for this organization, was small compared to many projects that are the subject of research. However, there was a complexity in the systemic inter-relationships between issues that arose, as discussed in Section 2.5.3. Capturing this systemicity, using mapping as a technique, gave explanations for some behaviors that were not obvious until the systemicity had been explored. One particular area explored was the interrelationship between two interdependent projects (the statement was made previously that lateness in one caused the other to overspend, but it was not clear as to why this happened). Mapping showed some of the root causes, how causal chains combined (so some issues exacerbated others), and how some rework positive feedback loops (Cooper [1993]) had been set up. The mapping also helped to explore some disagreements between project participants. It was also commented in the interviews that it would be important to capture systemicity within the organization, particularly because project managers tended to be external to the organization and these individuals would not be expecting systemic problems.

In addition to reviewing the lessons learned process, the process of collecting them was also studied. The literature survey in Chapter 2 identified many inhibiting factors to establishing useful lessons (such as lack of time, resources, incentives, or top management support) and identified internal formal lessons learned collection procedures as being an important factor facilitating learning. The survey of practice in Chapter 3 backed this last point up, with over 90% of the respondents believing that formal processes were important. It was perhaps necessary in this organization to revisit the process of how lessons were actually gathered.

One of the key issues for this organization was the inhibitions placed on the lessons learned process by issues of blame. This was highlighted in the literature survey in Chapter 2 (note that almost one half of the respondents in Chapter 3 felt that they avoided blame). In the case of this particular organization, this was magnified, due to the small size of the organization (in this case, some statements were difficult to make without revealing the identification of individuals), because of the typical UK civil-service care over what is written in texts, and also because of the management's relative power over outside project management contractors [who do not want to jeopardize their chances for future work]). This also contributed to making the end-of-project lessons learned reports more palliative. It was difficult from the outside to make a recommendation on how to circumvent this issue, which is partly cultural, but it does seem clear that the existence of the Centre of Excellence unit, perhaps with the power to offer anonymity, could be important here, both in preparing the lessons learned reports and in their dissemination role. It is worth remembering that the use of a specific department to oversee the lessons learned process (such as this Centre of Excellence) was indicated as valuable by approximately one half of the respondents in the survey in Chapter 3.

5.3 Conclusion

It was clear from the literature survey in Chapter 2 that the social process of narrative telling and recording can be an effective way to explore project issues and capture their complexity, whereas the straightforward noting of points and lessons learned may not be as effective (also this may be effective for capturing behaviors outside of the organizational norms). Similarly, 75% of survey respondents felt that the use of narratives was important. The types of lessons quoted in the lessons learned database in this case study would also clearly benefit from capturing the stories around the lessons to explain how the situation occurred and what the ramifications were. Again, it was difficult from the outside to make a recommendation about how to implement these benefits. The Centre of Excellence could point to relevant individuals for consultation, which was clearly of value; however, there were the issues of people leaving the organization and the availability of experiences held by outside project management contractors could not be relied upon. So how to actually make use of the benefits of narratives was not clear; it is worth remembering that in the survey in Chapter 3, this area showed one of the biggest disparities between "should" and "did," with only 17% of the organizations stating that they did actually make use of narratives (compared with the 75% who said it was important), although it is interesting that useful steps had been taken in this respect by Organization P in Chapter 4 (also a UK governmental body).

The final issue investigated was the dissemination of lessons learned throughout the organization, although issues of dissemination were slightly mitigated by the small size of the organization (although as noted above, this also exacerbated issues of "blame"). The survey in Chapter 3 suggested that project managers felt that this was one of the least successful aspects of the lessons learned process (and in this case, lessons need to be disseminated not just within the organization but also outside, since an external project management contractor would not know these lessons, particularly if they involved a different contractor). The literature survey clearly distinguished between two sets of techniques appropriate for knowledge dissemination, social methods (more appropriate for tacit knowledge), and IT-mediated methods (more appropriate for codifiable knowledge). The organization had set up a lessons learned database, the most common IT-mediated method; now, consideration needed to be given to how to disseminate lessons from the database. Clearly, the Centre of Excellence had an important role to play, primarily in pointing future project managers to the most relevant lessons learned and to reports and individuals who can supply context. Further consideration needed to be given to how future projects will have relevant issues brought to their attention. In terms of sharing of tacit knowledge, however, the mechanisms within the organization for disseminating tacit knowledge were not clear at all. The literature survey in Chapter 2 pointed to "communities of practice" as useful to share tacit knowledge, and it may be that if the project management community of practice within the organization were to be strengthened, sharing project experiences within that forum could help to preserve them. The role of the Centre of Excellence as a facilitator in addition to being a conduit of knowledge is important here.

6

CONCLUSIONS

This report has covered a range of activities, and summaries appear in the previous chapters. Specifically, a summary of the literature survey in Chapter 2 is given in Section 2.8, and a summary of the user-survey in Chapter 3 is given in Section 3.7. Some of the themes emerging from these summaries are briefly noted as follows:

- Learning lessons from project reviews is felt to be very important and an integral part of the learning organization. There was a good amount of support for further work in this area and improving practice.

- However, there was a wide disparity between what is done and what project managers feel should be done. Lack of employee time and lack of management support are leading reasons for lessons learned not being undertaken; a blame culture is a key inhibiting factor, to which so far there does not seem to be a general and useful answer. Formal processes seem to assist; however, the culture and structure of the organization are key factors inhibiting or facilitating the process.

- A specific department responsible for lessons learned is seen as useful.

- Getting to the root cause of project outcomes is a key issue in gathering lessons, and it can often be important to understand the complex systemicity underlying project outcomes to gain appropriate lessons.

- The social process of narrative telling and recording can be effective to explore project issues, capturing their complexity and behaviors outside of the organizational norms.

- One of the least successful aspects of learning is the transfer of lessons from the project team to the organization. Of the methods for knowledge dissemination, social methods are more appropriate for tacit knowledge and IT-mediated methods are more appropriate for codifiable knowledge. Within the former category, particularly for complex knowledge, there is increasing interest in Communities of Practice.

- Organizations differ radically in their requirements for lessons learned systems. The size of the organization, the size and complexity of their projects, their widespread geographical locations, and so on, all require different customizations of the methods for gathering and disseminating lessons. There is no "one size fits all" here.

Looking at the research questions outlined in Chapter 1 and asking "how far did we get in answering these questions?" we can conclude from all four chapters, notably the literature survey and particularly the survey of practice, the following:

1. This work has given us a good idea of what current practice looks like, and also what is generally considered to be best practice.

2. It is not clear whether current techniques have achieved their intended purpose. There were a variety of issues identified that need to be addressed.

3. Some techniques have been identified in previous chapters that will help to draw out difficult lessons from the projects.

4. Finally, the dissemination of lessons and the incorporation of lessons into organizational practice have received less attention in this brief study and clearly need further research.

APPENDIX 1
THE ZOOMERANG SURVEY

The Zoomerang survey appears as follows:

Learning through projects

Thank you for your interest in this survey. Your contribution to this research would be much appreciated.

The research is funded by the Project Management Institute (PMI) Research Program.

Learning through projects

The questions in this survey are about how organisations learn to manage projects better. This does not include learning about technical matters, or learning which is strictly personal.

A number of questions refer to "your organisation". For large organisations, you should consider this to be the extent which is governed by the same practices and processes for managing projects.

There are at most 32 questions in this survey.

Section 1. WHAT DOES YOUR ORGANISATION DO?

1   Does your organisation have any formal procedures or guidelines for learning lessons from projects?

2   Is there a specific department or unit which is responsible for supporting learning from projects?

     YES   NO

3   If yes, what is the main role of the department? Tick all that apply.

     ○ to capture learning from projects

     ○ to transfer learning to future projects

     ○ to audit the lessons learned process

     ○ to ensure compliance to standards

     ○ other

4   For which projects is there a "lessons learned" activity? Tick all that apply.

     ○ all projects

     ○ most projects

     ○ generally just big projects

     ○ generally just successful projects

     ○ generally just unsuccessful projects

     ○ ad hoc after some projects

     ○ none

     ○ other, please specify

Learning through projects

5   When there is a "lessons learned" activity, at what stage of the project does it happen? Tick all that apply.

   ○ when the project has been completed
   ○ on completion of major milestones or deliverables
   ○ at regular intervals e.g. monthly
   ○ when a problem arises
   ○ when generated by a business need
   ○ on an ad hoc basis

6   Who is usually involved? Tick all that apply.

   ○ project management staff
   ○ technical staff
   ○ financial staff
   ○ contract / legal staff
   ○ senior management
   ○ HRM staff
   ○ customers
   ○ subcontractors

7   Which of the following does your organisation do to capture lessons from projects? Tick all that apply.

   ○ meetings / workshops for those involved
   ○ individual interviews
   ○ project audits / health checks
   ○ learning diaries / logs
   ○ learning histories / narratives
   ○ seek views of the public / customers
   ○ process coordinated by a project-external facilitator
   ○ process conducted by a project-external team
   ○ other, please specify

8   Which of the following does your organisation use to transfer lessons outside the project team? Tick all that apply.

   ○ corporate training
   ○ individuals moving on to new projects

- IT mediated methods e.g. database
- learning histories / narratives
- learning networks / communities of practice
- learning resources centre
- mentoring
- presentations and conferences
- short micro-articles or video clips
- writing lessons into company procedures
- written documentation
- ad hoc
- other, please specify

9   Are there any other ways project teams can access lessons from previous projects?

SUBMIT

Learning through projects

Section 2. HOW SUCCESSFUL ARE YOUR PROCESSES?

10 How good are your processes for learning from projects?

	1 strongly agree	2 tend to agree	3 tend to disagree	4 strongly disagree	N/A
We are able to identify clear issues	1	2	3	4	
We are able to prioritise issues	1	2	3	4	
We avoid issues of blame	1	2	3	4	
People are willing to share learning about project failures	1	2	3	4	
We get to the root-causes of project outcomes, e.g. systemic cause-effect relationships	1	2	3	4	

11 How useful would you say are the lessons you learn?

	1 strongly agree	2 tend to agree	3 tend to disagree	4 strongly disagree	N/A
We learn complex lessons as well as simple lessons	1	2	3	4	
The lessons are generalisable to other projects	1	2	3	4	
We create knowledge rather than simply collecting data	1	2	3	4	
We achieve outputs that are truthful	1	2	3	4	

12 Which of these have your lessons learned processes achieved?

	1 strongly agree	2 tend to agree	3 tend to disagree	4 strongly disagree	N/A
Projects are more successful	1	2	3	4	
The project competency within the organisation has increased	1	2	3	4	
My own competency as a project manager has increased	1	2	3	4	

SUBMIT ➤

Learning through projects

13   Are your learning processes measured for effectiveness?

[YES] [NO]

If yes, then how?

```
┌──────────────────────────────────────────────┐▲
│                                              │
│                                              │
│                                              │▼
└──────────────────────────────────────────────┘
```

14   Do you benchmark your processes for learning from projects?

[YES] [NO]

15   If yes, whose learning processes do you use for benchmarking?

○ similar projects within the organisation

○ dissimilar projects within the organisation

○ other organisations within the same industry

○ organisations in other industries

16   How well are lessons transferred through the organisation?

1 strongly agree	2 tend to agree	3 tend to disagree	4 don't know	N/A
Lessons learned move effectively beyond the individual to the project team				
[1]	[2]	[3]	[4]	[ ]
Lessons learned move effectively beyond the project team to the organisation				
[1]	[2]	[3]	[4]	[ ]
Lessons learned are applied by other project teams				
[1]	[2]	[3]	[4]	[ ]
(International organisations only) Learning is achieved across cultures				
[1]	[2]	[3]	[4]	[ ]

17   How often are lessons learned from projects implemented into the organisation's processes?

routinely	sometimes	rarely or never
[1]	[2]	[3]

18   Has the organisation ever changed its strategy because of the lessons learned process?

yes, often	yes, at least once	no

Learning through projects

Section 3. WHAT DO YOU THINK IS BEST PRACTICE?

19 Which of the following practices do you think your organisation should be doing to learn lessons from projects?

1 very important	2 important	3 useful but not essential	4 not useful

Use a formal procedure for lessons learned

| 1 | 2 | 3 | 4 |

Have a specific department which is responsible for doing lessons learned

| 1 | 2 | 3 | 4 |

Collect and review lessons at all stages of the project life cycle

| 1 | 2 | 3 | 4 |

Hold meetings / workshops for those involved

| 1 | 2 | 3 | 4 |

Surface issues in a public forum

| 1 | 2 | 3 | 4 |

Interview people individually

| 1 | 2 | 3 | 4 |

Conduct regular project audits / health checks

| 1 | 2 | 3 | 4 |

Keep learning diaries / logs during the project

| 1 | 2 | 3 | 4 |

Construct a learning history / narrative of the project after the event

| 1 | 2 | 3 | 4 |

Process is coordinated by a project-external facilitator

| 1 | 2 | 3 | 4 |

Process is conducted by a project-external team

| 1 | 2 | 3 | 4 |

20 Are there any other practices you think your organisation should be doing to learn lessons from projects?

21 Which do you think your organisation should be doing to transfer lessons learned to future projects?

1 very important	2 important	3 useful but not essential	4 not useful

Store lessons learned in a well-indexed database

| 1 | 2 | 3 | 4 |

Construct a learning history / narrative of the project after the event

| 1 | 2 | 3 | 4 |

Encourage learning networks / communities of practice

| 1 | 2 | 3 | 4 |

Put together short micro-articles or video clips of lessons learned

| 1 | 2 | 3 | 4 |

Train individuals in retrieving and tailoring lessons learned

| 1 | 2 | 3 | 4 |

Have a specific department responsible for retrieving lessons learned

| 1 | 2 | 3 | 4 |

22 Are there any ways in which access to lessons learned from previous projects could be made easier?

SUBMIT

Learning through projects

Section 4. WHAT STOPS YOU DOING MORE?

23 What hinders people in your organisation from putting more effort into
the lessons-learned process (capture and transfer)?

- we already put in enough effort
- lack of clear guidelines
- lack of employee time
- lack of resources
- lack of incentive
- lack of management support
- lack of support from others in the organisation
- the wrong participants are involved
- our processes don't capture useful lessons
- the lessons are not transferable to other projects
- the data repository is too hard to search
- other, please specify

24 Do you feel that more "stories" or case studies would be of significant
value?

[YES] [NO]

[SUBMIT]

Learning through projects

Section 5. DEMOGRAPHICS

25   How many years experience do you have of managing projects?

[▼]

26   To which professional bodies are you affiliated?

- ⦿ PMI
- ⦿ an APFPM organisation
- ⦿ an IPMA organisation
- ⦿ APM (UK)
- ⦿ AIPM (Australia)
- ⦿ other
- ⦿ none

27   Do you have a professional project management qualification?

- ⦿ No
- ⦿ Yes, PMP
- ⦿ Yes, other

SUBMIT ➤

Learning through projects

28 Which of these best describes your organisation's industry?

29 How many employees (full-time equivalent) are there in your organisation?

30 Roughly what proportion of the total work in your organisation is done in a project orientation?

31 What is the average size of projects in your organisation, measured in US dollars?

32 Which of the following best describes the maturity of project management in your organisation? Project management is:

SUBMIT

Thank you for taking our survey

 Project Management Institute
® Building professionalism in project management. ®

 POWERED BY

Copyright ©1999-2005 MarketTools, Inc. All Rights Reserved.
No portion of this site may be copied without the express written consent of MarketTools, Inc.

APPENDIX 2
THE ZOOMERANG RESULTS

The results of the Zoomerang survey are as follows:

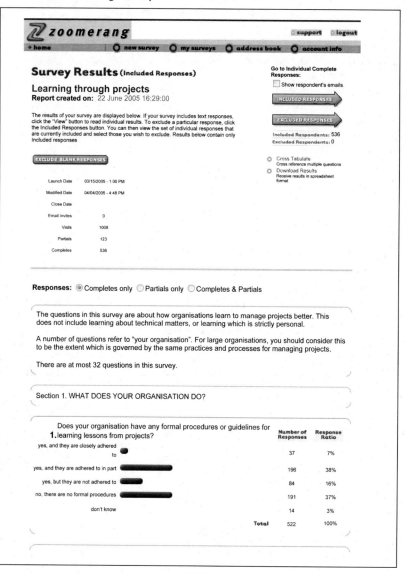

2. Is there a specific department or unit which is responsible for supporting learning from projects?

	Number of Responses	Response Ratio
Yes	165	32%
No	356	68%
Total	521	100%

3. If yes, what is the main role of the department? Tick all that apply.

	Number of Responses	Response Ratio
to capture learning from projects	99	56%
to transfer learning to future projects	78	44%
to audit the lessons learned process	44	25%
to ensure compliance to standards	88	50%
other	32	18%

4. For which projects is there a "lessons learned" activity? Tick all that apply.

	Number of Responses	Response Ratio
all projects	79	16%
most projects	104	20%
generally just big projects	116	23%
generally just successful projects	12	2%
generally just unsuccessful projects	40	8%
ad hoc after some projects	160	31%
none	48	9%
VIEW other, please specify	21	4%

5. When there is a "lessons learned" activity, at what stage of the project does it happen? Tick all that apply.

	Number of Responses	Response Ratio
when the project has been completed	352	75%
on completion of major milestones or deliverables	85	18%
at regular intervals e.g. monthly	21	4%
when a problem arises	78	17%
when generated by a business need	26	6%
on an ad hoc basis	92	20%

6. Who is usually involved? Tick all that apply.

	Number of Responses	Response Ratio
project management staff	441	95%
technical staff	325	70%
financial staff	52	11%

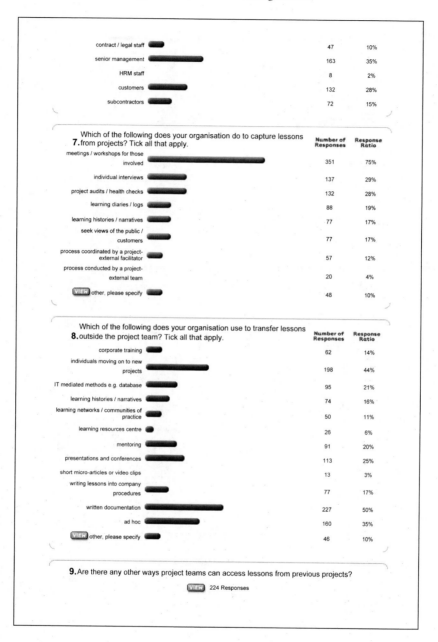

	Number of Responses	Response Ratio
contract / legal staff	47	10%
senior management	163	35%
HRM staff	8	2%
customers	132	28%
subcontractors	72	15%

7. Which of the following does your organisation do to capture lessons from projects? Tick all that apply.

	Number of Responses	Response Ratio
meetings / workshops for those involved	351	75%
individual interviews	137	29%
project audits / health checks	132	28%
learning diaries / logs	88	19%
learning histories / narratives	77	17%
seek views of the public / customers	77	17%
process coordinated by a project-external facilitator	57	12%
process conducted by a project-external team	20	4%
other, please specify	48	10%

8. Which of the following does your organisation use to transfer lessons outside the project team? Tick all that apply.

	Number of Responses	Response Ratio
corporate training	62	14%
individuals moving on to new projects	198	44%
IT mediated methods e.g. database	95	21%
learning histories / narratives	74	16%
learning networks / communities of practice	50	11%
learning resources centre	26	6%
mentoring	91	20%
presentations and conferences	113	25%
short micro-articles or video clips	13	3%
writing lessons into company procedures	77	17%
written documentation	227	50%
ad hoc	160	35%
other, please specify	46	10%

9. Are there any other ways project teams can access lessons from previous projects?

224 Responses

Section 2. HOW SUCCESSFUL ARE YOUR PROCESSES?

10. How good are your processes for learning from projects?

The top percentage indicates total respondent ratio; the bottom number represents actual number of respondents selecting the option	1 strongly agree	2 tend to agree	3 tend to disagree	4 strongly disagree	N/A
1. We are able to identify clear issues	12% 56	55% 259	24% 113	8% 40	1% 4
2. We are able to prioritise issues	8% 40	49% 232	31% 144	10% 48	2% 8
3. We avoid issues of blame	16% 76	40% 190	27% 129	15% 69	2% 8
4. People are willing to share learning about project failures	13% 60	44% 207	32% 152	10% 47	1% 4
5. We get to the root-causes of project outcomes, e.g. systemic cause-effect relationships	7% 31	33% 156	38% 179	20% 96	2% 8

11. How useful would you say are the lessons you learn?

The top percentage indicates total respondent ratio; the bottom number represents actual number of respondents selecting the option	1 strongly agree	2 tend to agree	3 tend to disagree	4 strongly disagree	N/A
1. We learn complex lessons as well as simple lessons	10% 49	46% 214	33% 157	8% 38	3% 12
2. The lessons are generalisable to other projects	15% 68	55% 256	23% 109	6% 27	2% 8
3. We create knowledge rather than simply collecting data	11% 54	33% 153	37% 172	17% 82	2% 9
4. We achieve outputs that are truthful	10% 47	57% 268	25% 117	6% 30	1% 7

12. Which of these have your lessons learned processes achieved?

The top percentage indicates total respondent ratio; the bottom number represents actual number of respondents selecting the option	1 strongly agree	2 tend to agree	3 tend to disagree	4 strongly disagree	N/A
1. Projects are more successful	8% 37	44% 208	37% 173	6% 27	5% 25
2. The project competency within the organisation has increased	11% 51	48% 223	30% 140	8% 37	4% 17
3. My own competency as a project manager has increased	29% 135	55% 257	11% 50	2% 10	4% 17

13. Are your learning processes measured for effectiveness?

	Number of Responses	Response Ratio
Yes	42	9%
No	422	91%
Total	464	100%

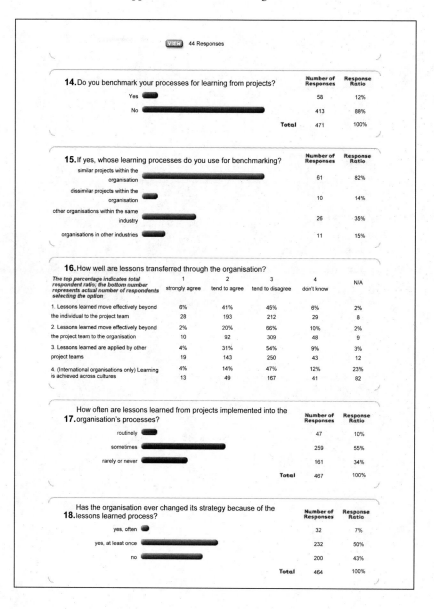

VIEW 44 Responses

14. Do you benchmark your processes for learning from projects?

	Number of Responses	Response Ratio
Yes	58	12%
No	413	88%
Total	471	100%

15. If yes, whose learning processes do you use for benchmarking?

	Number of Responses	Response Ratio
similar projects within the organisation	61	82%
dissimilar projects within the organisation	10	14%
other organisations within the same industry	26	35%
organisations in other industries	11	15%

16. How well are lessons transferred through the organisation?

The top percentage indicates total respondent ratio; the bottom number represents actual number of respondents selecting the option	1 strongly agree	2 tend to agree	3 tend to disagree	4 don't know	N/A
1. Lessons learned move effectively beyond the individual to the project team	6% / 28	41% / 193	45% / 212	6% / 29	2% / 8
2. Lessons learned move effectively beyond the project team to the organisation	2% / 10	20% / 92	66% / 309	10% / 48	2% / 9
3. Lessons learned are applied by other project teams	4% / 19	31% / 143	54% / 250	9% / 43	3% / 12
4. (International organisations only) Learning is achieved across cultures	4% / 13	14% / 49	47% / 167	12% / 41	23% / 82

17. How often are lessons learned from projects implemented into the organisation's processes?

	Number of Responses	Response Ratio
routinely	47	10%
sometimes	259	55%
rarely or never	161	34%
Total	467	100%

18. Has the organisation ever changed its strategy because of the lessons learned process?

	Number of Responses	Response Ratio
yes, often	32	7%
yes, at least once	232	50%
no	200	43%
Total	464	100%

Section 3. WHAT DO YOU THINK IS BEST PRACTICE?

19. Which of the following practices do you think your organisation should be doing to learn lessons from projects?

The top percentage indicates total respondent ratio; the bottom number represents actual number of respondents selecting the option	1 very important	2 important	3 useful but not essential	4 not useful
1. Use a formal procedure for lessons learned	50% 255	43% 220	7% 36	1% 4
2. Have a specific department which is responsible for doing lessons learned	17% 86	30% 154	41% 212	12% 61
3. Collect and review lessons at all stages of the project life cycle	38% 193	46% 235	15% 79	1% 7
4. Hold meetings / workshops for those involved	42% 213	47% 242	11% 54	1% 4
5. Surface issues in a public forum	18% 91	39% 199	35% 178	8% 43
6. Interview people individually	18% 90	44% 228	34% 177	4% 19
7. Conduct regular project audits / health checks	40% 201	47% 237	12% 61	2% 8
8. Keep learning diaries / logs during the project	30% 154	45% 231	22% 114	2% 10
9. Construct a learning history / narrative of the project after the event	31% 156	44% 226	21% 109	4% 18
10. Process is coordinated by a project-external facilitator	16% 82	30% 151	39% 200	15% 75
11. Process is conducted by a project-external team	7% 36	24% 120	47% 241	22% 112

20. Are there any other practices you think your organisation should be doing to learn lessons from projects?

VIEW 169 Responses

21. Which do you think your organisation should be doing to transfer lessons learned to future projects?

The top percentage indicates total respondent ratio; the bottom number represents actual number of respondents selecting the option	1 very important	2 important	3 useful but not essential	4 not useful
1. Store lessons learned in a well-indexed database	49% 251	38% 197	11% 58	2% 9
2. Construct a learning history / narrative of the project after the event	30% 154	49% 251	19% 100	2% 11
3. Encourage learning networks / communities of practice	47% 243	41% 212	10% 52	1% 5
4. Put together short micro-articles or video clips of lessons learned	14% 73	32% 163	45% 232	9% 44
5. Train individuals in retrieving and tailoring lessons learned	36% 185	48% 247	15% 75	1% 7
6. Have a specific department responsible	14%	32%	39%	15%

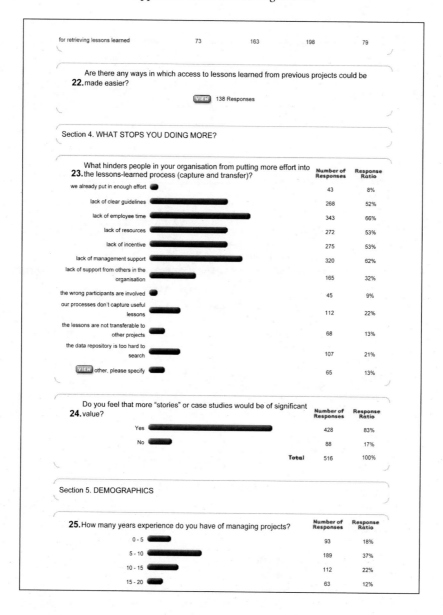

for retrieving lessons learned   73   163   198   79

22. Are there any ways in which access to lessons learned from previous projects could be made easier?

VIEW 138 Responses

Section 4. WHAT STOPS YOU DOING MORE?

23. What hinders people in your organisation from putting more effort into the lessons-learned process (capture and transfer)?

	Number of Responses	Response Ratio
we already put in enough effort	43	8%
lack of clear guidelines	268	52%
lack of employee time	343	66%
lack of resources	272	53%
lack of incentive	275	53%
lack of management support	320	62%
lack of support from others in the organisation	165	32%
the wrong participants are involved	45	9%
our processes don't capture useful lessons	112	22%
the lessons are not transferable to other projects	68	13%
the data repository is too hard to search	107	21%
VIEW other, please specify	65	13%

24. Do you feel that more "stories" or case studies would be of significant value?

	Number of Responses	Response Ratio
Yes	428	83%
No	88	17%
Total	516	100%

Section 5. DEMOGRAPHICS

25. How many years experience do you have of managing projects?

	Number of Responses	Response Ratio
0 - 5	93	18%
5 - 10	189	37%
10 - 15	112	22%
15 - 20	63	12%

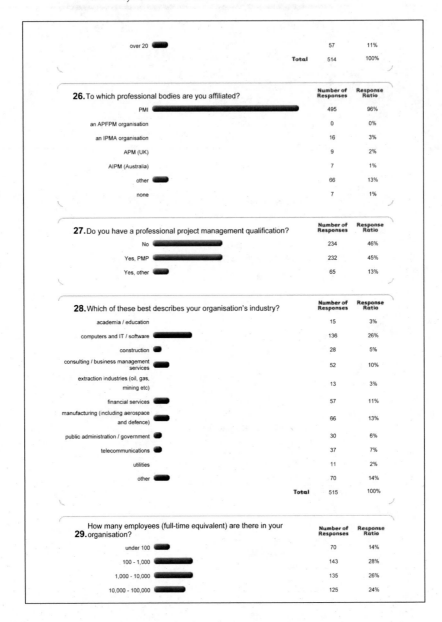

	Number of Responses	Response Ratio
over 20	57	11%
Total	514	100%

26. To which professional bodies are you affiliated?

	Number of Responses	Response Ratio
PMI	495	96%
an APFPM organisation	0	0%
an IPMA organisation	16	3%
APM (UK)	9	2%
AIPM (Australia)	7	1%
other	66	13%
none	7	1%

27. Do you have a professional project management qualification?

	Number of Responses	Response Ratio
No	234	46%
Yes, PMP	232	45%
Yes, other	65	13%

28. Which of these best describes your organisation's industry?

	Number of Responses	Response Ratio
academia / education	15	3%
computers and IT / software	136	26%
construction	28	5%
consulting / business management services	52	10%
extraction industries (oil, gas, mining etc)	13	3%
financial services	57	11%
manufacturing (including aerospace and defence)	66	13%
public administration / government	30	6%
telecommunications	37	7%
utilities	11	2%
other	70	14%
Total	515	100%

29. How many employees (full-time equivalent) are there in your organisation?

	Number of Responses	Response Ratio
under 100	70	14%
100 - 1,000	143	28%
1,000 - 10,000	135	26%
10,000 - 100,000	125	24%

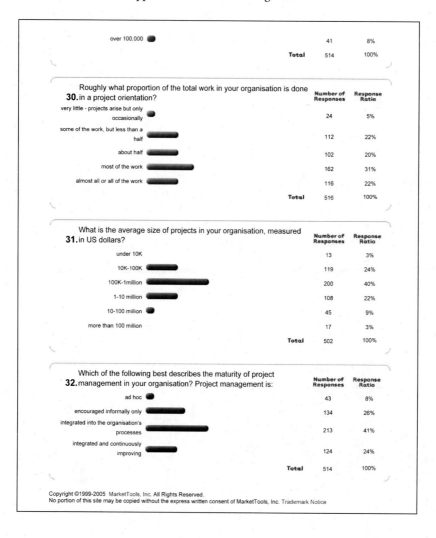

	Number of Responses	Response Ratio
over 100,000	41	8%
Total	514	100%

30. Roughly what proportion of the total work in your organisation is done in a project orientation?

	Number of Responses	Response Ratio
very little - projects arise but only occasionally	24	5%
some of the work, but less than a half	112	22%
about half	102	20%
most of the work	162	31%
almost all or all of the work	116	22%
Total	516	100%

31. What is the average size of projects in your organisation, measured in US dollars?

	Number of Responses	Response Ratio
under 10K	13	3%
10K-100K	119	24%
100K-1million	200	40%
1-10 million	108	22%
10-100 million	45	9%
more than 100 million	17	3%
Total	502	100%

32. Which of the following best describes the maturity of project management in your organisation? Project management is:

	Number of Responses	Response Ratio
ad hoc	43	8%
encouraged informally only	134	26%
integrated into the organisation's processes	213	41%
integrated and continuously improving	124	24%
Total	514	100%

Companies where project management is more mature (integrated or mature) are more likely to agree with all statements relating to the success of the lessons learned process with the exception of "my competency as a project manager has increased." (Note that most figures are lower than the corresponding figures in the table comparing agreement by adherence to formal procedures; that is correct and arises because of the greater number of companies where project management is mature or integrated than those that have and adhere to formal procedures.)

Quality Of Processes	Tend to Agree or Strongly Agree, %	
	(A)*	(B)*
Lessons are generalizable to other projects (11b)	74.1	62.8
Outputs are truthful (11d)	75.1	52.7
We identify clear issues (10a)	73.0	56.7
We prioritize issues (10b)	65.9	43.8
We learn complex lessons (11a)	63.1	45.5
We avoid blame (10c)	62.7	45.6
People share learning about failures (10d)	64.1	41.5
We create knowledge rather than simply collecting data (11c)	50.3	33.6
We get to the root causes of project outcomes (10e)	47.9	25.9
Results of Lessons Learned	**Tend to Agree or Strongly Agree, %**	
	(A)	(B)
My competency as a project manager has increased (12c)	87.8	83.8
Project competency within the organization has increased (12b)	66.4	50.0
Projects are more successful (12a)	58.5	47.4
Transfer of Lessons Learned	**Tend to Agree or Strongly Agree, %**	
	(A)	(B)
Lessons learned move from the individual to the project team (16a)	57.6	26.7
Lessons learned are applied by other project teams (16c)	42.5	21.4
Learning is achieved across cultures (16d)	28.3	11.3
Lessons learned move from the project team to the organization (16b)	28.1	9.0

*Column A represents companies where project management is mature or integrated
Column B represents companies where project management is encouraged or ad hoc

Figure A3-1 **Summary of Results**

REFERENCES

Abma, T. A. 2003. Learning by telling: Storytelling workshops as an organizational learning intervention. *Management Learning* 34:221–40.

Abramovici, A. 1999. Gathering and using lessons learned. *PM Network* 30(10):61–63.

Ackermann, F., C. Eden, and T. Williams. 1997. Modelling for litigation: Mixing qualitative and quantitative approaches. *Interfaces* 27:48–65.

Ambrosini, V., and C. Bowman. 2001. Tacit knowledge: Some suggestions for operationalization. *Journal of Management Studies* 38:811–29.

Ancori, B., A. Bureth, and P. Cohendet. 2000. The economics of knowledge: The debate about codification and tacit knowledge. *Industrial and Corporate Change* 9:255–87.

Anderson, A. 2000. The introduction of virtual team-working in the automotive supply chain. Paper presented at the ESRC Innovation Programme, End of Programme Conference, Cranfield, Beds, UK.

Arthur, M. B., R. J. DeFillippi, and C. Jones. 2001. Project-based learning as the interplay of career and company non-financial capital. *Management Learning* 32:99–117.

Ayas, K. 1996. Professional project management: A shift towards learning and a knowledge creating structure. *International Journal of Project Management* 14:131–36.

Ayas, K. 1998. Learning through projects: Meeting the implementation challenge. In *Projects as arenas for renewal and learning processes*, ed. R. Lundin and C. Midler, 89–98. Dordrecht, The Netherlands: Kluwer Academic Publishers.

Ayas, K., and N. Zeniuk. 2001. Project-based learning: Building communities of reflective practitioners. *Management Learning* 32:61–76.

Azzone, G., and P. Maccarrone. 2001. The design of the investment post-audit process in large organisations: Evidence from a survey. *European Journal of Innovation Management* 4:73–87.

Bapuji, H., and M. Crossan. 2004. From questions to answers: Reviewing organizational learning research. *Management Learning* 35:397–417.

Barker, M., and K. Neailey. 1999. From individual learning to project team learning and innovation: A structured approach. *Journal of Workplace Learning* 11:60–67.

Barnes, N. M., and S. H. Wearne. 1993. The future for major project management. *International Journal of Project Management* 11:135–42.

Baumard, P. 1999. *Tacit knowledge in Organizations*. London: Sage Publications.

Berke, M. F. 2001. Best practices lessons learned (BPLL): A view from the trenches. *Proceedings of the PMI Seminars and Symposium 2001*, CD-ROM. Newtown Square, PA: Project Management Institute.

Besner, C., and B. Hobbs. 2004. An empirical investigation of project management practice: In reality, which tools do practitioners use? *Proceedings of the PMI Research Conference 2004*, CD-ROM. Newtown Square, PA: Project Management Institute.

Blackler, F., N. Crump, and S. McDonald. 1998. Knowledge, organizations and competition. In *Knowing in firms: Understanding, managing and measuring knowledge*, ed. G. von Krogh, J. Roos, and D. Kleine, 67–86. London: Sage Publications.

Boddy, D., and R. Paton. 2004. Responding to competing narratives: Lessons for project managers. *International Journal of Project Management* 22:225–33.

Boje, D. M. 1991. The storytelling organisation: A study of story performance in an office-supply firm. *Administrative Science Quarterly* 36:106–26.

Boje, D. M. 1995. Stories of the storytelling organization: A postmodern analysis of Disney as "Tamara-Land." *Academy of Management Journal* 38(4):997–1036.

Bosch-Sijtsema, P. M. 2002. Knowledge management in virtual organisations: Interorganisational and interproject knowledge transfer. *Proceedings of OKLC 2002: The Third European Conference on Organizational Knowledge, Learning and Capabilities, Session 12-7*, Athens, Greece. Athens, Greece: Athens Laboratory of Business Administration.

Bourne, L., and D. H. T. Walker. 2004. Advancing project management in learning organizations. *The Learning Organization* 11:226–43.

Boyce, M. E. 1996. Organizational story and storytelling: A critical review. *Journal of Organizational Change Management* 9:5–26.

Brady, T., and A. Davies. 2004. Building project capabilities: From exploratory to exploitative learning. *Organization Studies* 25:1601–22.

Brady, T., N. Marshall, A. Prencipe, and F. Tell. 2002. Making sense of learning landscapes in project-based organisations. *Proceedings of OKLC 2002: The Third European Conference on Organizational Knowledge, Learning and Capabilities, Session 13-3*, Athens, Greece. Athens, Greece: Athens Laboratory of Business Administration.

Brander-Löf, I., J.-U. Hilger, and C. André. 2000. How to learn from projects: The work improvement review. *Proceedings of the IPMA World Congress*. Zurich: International Project Management Association 2000.

Bredillet, C. N. 2004a. Projects are producing the knowledge which are producing the projects. *Proceedings of the IPMA World Congress*.

Bredillet, C. N. 2004b. Understanding the very nature of project management: A praxiological approach. *Proceedings of the PMI Research Conference 2004*, CD-ROM. Newtown Square, PA: Project Management Institute.

Bresnen, M., L. Edelman, S. Newell, H. Scarbrough, and J. Swan. 2003. Social practices and the management of knowledge in project environments. *International Journal of Project Management* 21:157–66.

Bresnen, M., L. Edelman, J. Swan, S. Laurent, H. Scarbrough, and S. Newell. 2002. Cross-sector research on knowledge management practices for project-based learning. *Proceedings of EURAM 2002: Innovative Research in Management.* Brussels: EURAM 2002.

Bresnen, M., A. Goussevskaia, and J. Swan. 2004. Embedding new management knowledge in project-based organizations. *Organization Studies* 25:1535–55.

Brown, A. D., and M. R. Jones. 1998. Doomed to failure: Narratives of inevitability and conspiracy in a failed IS project. *Organization Studies* 19:73–88.

Brown, J. S., and P. Duguid. 1991. Organizational learning and communities-of-practice: Toward a unified view of working, learning and innovation. *Organization Science* 2:40–57.

Brown, P. 2004. A cure that harms? The enactment of project management on IS projects. Paper presented at the 2nd International Workshop, "Making Projects Critical." Bristol, UK: University of the West of England 2004.

Bukszar, E., and T. Connolly. 1988. Hindsight bias and strategic choice: Some problems in learning from experience. *Academy of Management Journal* 31:628-41.

Bullard, T. M. 2005. Project management "train wrecks" – How to ensure your project is on the right track! *Proceedings of the PMI Global Congress 2005—EMEA,* CD-ROM. Newtown Square, PA: Project Management Institute.

Busby, J. S. 1999a. An assessment of post-project reviews. *Project Management Journal* 30:23–29.

Busby, J. S. 1999b. The effectiveness of collective retrospection as a mechanism of organizational learning. *The Journal of Applied Behavioral Science* 35:109–29.

Carmona, S., and A. Grönlund. 1998. Learning from forgetting: An experiential study of two European car manufacturers. *Management Learning* 29:21–38.

Carrillo, P. 2004. Managing knowledge: Lessons from the oil and gas sector. *Construction Management and Economics* 22:631–42.

Carrillo, P., H. Robinson, A. Al-Ghassani, and C. Anumba. 2004. Knowledge management in UK construction: strategies, resources and barriers. *Project Management Journal* 35:46–56.

Cassells, E. 1999. Building a learning organization in the offshore oil industry. *Long Range Planning* 32:245–52.

Cavaleri, S.A., and D. S. Fearon. 2000. Integrating organizational learning and business praxis: A case for intelligent project management. *The Learning Organization* 7:251–58.

Cicmil, S. 2005. Reflection, participation and learning in project environments: A multiple perspective agenda. In *Knowledge management in project environments,* ed. P. Love, Z. Irani, and P. Fong. Oxford: Elsevier / Butterworth-Heinemann, 155–80.

Cole-Gomolski, B. 1997. Users loath to share their know-how. *Computerworld* 31:6.

Collier, B., T. DeMarco, and P. Fearey. 1996. A defined process for project post-mortem review. *IEEE Software* 13:65–72.

Collison, C., and G. Parcell. 2001. *Learning to fly – Practical lessons from one the world's leading knowledge companies.* Oxford: Capstone Publishing.

Connell, N. A. D., J. H. Klein, and E. Meyer. 2004. Narrative approaches to the transfer of organisational knowledge. *Knowledge Management Research and Practice* 2:184–93.

Connell, N. A. D., J. H. Klein, and P. L. Powell. 2003. It's tacit knowledge but not as we know it: Redirecting the search for knowledge. *Journal of the Operational Research Society* 54:140–52.

Cook, S. D. N., and J. S. Brown. 1999. Bridging epistemologies: The generative dance between organizational knowledge and organizational knowing. *Organization Science* 10:381–400.

Cooke-Davies, T. 1996. Learning in a project-based organisation. *Proceedings of the IPMA 96 World Congress on Project Management*. Zurich: International Project Management Association 2000.

Cooke-Davies, T. 2002. The "real" success factors on projects. *International Journal of Project Management* 20:185–90.

Cooke-Davies, T., and A. Arzymanow. 2002. The maturity of project management in different industries. *Proceedings of IRNOP 5: Fifth International Conference of the International Research Network of Organizing by Projects*. East Horsley, UK: EuroProjex Ltd.

Coombs, R., and R. Hull. 1998. "Knowledge management practices" and path-dependency in innovation. *Research Policy* 27:237–53.

Cooper, K. 1993. The rework cycle: benchmarks for the project manager. *Project Management Journal* 20:17–21.

Cooper, K. 1994. The $2000 hour: How managers influence project performance through the rework cycle. *Project Management Journal* 25:11–24.

Cooper, K. G., J. M. Lyneis, and B. J. Bryant. 2002. Learning to learn, from past to future. *International Journal of Project Management* 20:213–19.

Coutu, D. L. 2002. The anxiety of learning. *Harvard Business Review* 80:100.

Crawford, L., J. B. Hobbs, and J. R. Turner. 2004. Project categorization systems and their use in organizations: An empirical study. *Proceedings of the PMI Research Conference 2004*, CD-ROM. Newtown Square, PA: Project Management Institute.

Crosman, L. 2002. Lessons learned – The army way. *Proceedings of the PMI Seminars and Symposium 2002*, CD-ROM. Newtown Square, PA: Project Management Institute.

Cross, R., and L. Baird. 2000. Technology is not enough: Improving performance by building organizational memory. *Sloan Management Review* 41:69–78.

Crossan, M. M., H. W. Lane, and R. E. White. 1999. An organisational learning framework: From intuition to institution. *Academy of Management: The Academy of Management Review* 24:522–37.

Davies, A., and T. Brady. 2000. Organisational capabilities and learning in complex product systems: Towards repeatable solutions. *Research Policy* 29:931–53.

Deane, R. H., T. B. Clark, and D. Young. 1997. Creating a learning project environment: Aligning project outcomes with customer needs. *Information Systems Management* 14:55–60.

DeFillippi, R. J. 2001. Introduction: Project-based learning, reflective practices and learning outcomes. *Management Learning* 32:5–10.

DeFillippi, R. J., and M. B. Arthur. 1998. Paradox in project-based enterprise: The case of film-making. *California Management Review* 40:125–39.

DeFillippi, R. J., and M. B. Arthur. 2002. Project-based learning, embedded learning contexts and the management of knowledge. *Proceedings of OKLC 2002: The Third European Conference on Organizational Knowledge, Learning and Capabilities, Session 13-11*, Athens, Greece. Athens, Greece: Athens Laboratory of Business Administration.

Delisle, C. L. 2004. Communities of practice: Ingenuity in the Canadian federal government. *Proceedings of the PMI Research Conference 2004*, CD-ROM. Newtown Square, PA: Project Management Institute.

Denrell, J. 2003. Vicarious learning, undersampling of failure, and the myths of management. *Organization Science* 14:227–43.

Desouza, K. C. 2003. Facilitating tacit knowledge exchange. *Communications of the ACM* 46:85–88.

DiBella, A. J., and E. C. Nevis. 1998. *How organizations learn*. Hoboken, NJ: Jossey-Bass.

Dierkes, M., A. Berthoin-Antal, J. Child, and I. N. Nonaka. 2001. *The handbook of organizational knowledge*. Oxford: Oxford University Press.

Disterer, G. 2002. Management of project knowledge and experiences. *Journal of Knowledge Management* 6:512–20.

Dodgson, M. 1993. Organizational learning: A review of some literatures. *Organization Studies* 14:375–94.

Easterby-Smith, M., R. Thorpe, and A. Lowe. 1991. *Management research: An introduction*. London: Sage Publications.

Easterby-Smith, M., M. Crossan, and D. Nicolini. 2000. Organizational learning: Debates past, present and future. *Journal of Management Studies* 37:783–96.

Eden, C., F. Ackermann, and T. Williams. 2005. The amoebic growth of project costs. *Project Management Journal* 36:15–27.

Eden, C., T. Williams, F. Ackermann, and S. Howick. 2000. On the nature of disruption and delay (D&D) in major projects. *Journal of the Operational Research Society* 51:291–300.

Edmondson, A. C. 2002. The local and variegated nature of learning in organizations: A group-level perspective. *Organization Science* 13:128–46.

Edmondson, A., and B. Moingeon. 1998. From organizational learning to the learning organization. *Management Learning* 29:5–20.

Ekstedt, E., R. A. Lundinm, A. Soderholm, and H. Wirdenius. 1999. *Neo-industrial organising: Renewal by action and knowledge formation in a project-intensive economy*. London: Routledge.

Englund, R. L., and R. J. Graham. 1999. From experience: Linking projects to strategy. *Journal of Product Innovation Management* 16:52–64.

Eppler, M., and O. Sukowski. 2000. Managing team knowledge: Core processes, tools and enabling factors. *European Management Journal* 18:334–341.

Fernie, S., S. D. Green, S. J. Weller, and R. Newcombe. 2003. Knowledge sharing: Context, confusion and controversy. *International Journal of Project Management* 21:177–87.

Fong, P. 2002. Knowledge creation in multidisciplinary project teams: An empirical study of the processes and their dynamic interrelationships. *Proceedings of IRNOP 5: Fifth International Conference of the International Research Network of Organizing by Projects*. East Horsley, UK: EuroProjex Ltd.

Fong, P. S. W. 2005. Managing knowledge in project-based professional services firms: An international comparison. In *Knowledge management in project environments*, ed. P. Love, Z. Irani, and P. Fong. Oxford: Elsevier / Butterworth-Heinemann 103–32.

Fortune, J., and G. Peters. 1995. *Learning from failure: The systems approach*. Chichester, UK: Wiley.

Franco, L. A., M. Cushman, and J. Rosenhead. 2004. Project review and learning in the construction industry: Embedding a problem structuring method within a partnership context. *European Journal of Operational Research* 152:586–601.

Gabriel, Y. 2000. *Storytelling in organisations: Facts, fictions and fantasies*. Oxford: Oxford University Press.

Gann, D. M., and A. J. Salter. 2000. Innovation in project-based, service-enhanced firms: The construction of complex products and systems. *Research Policy* 29:955–72.

Garnett, N., and S. Pickrell. 2000. Benchmarking for construction: Theory and practice. *Construction Management and Economics* 18:55–63.

Garrety, K., P. L. Robertson, and R. Badham. 2004. Integrating communities of practice in technology development projects. *International Journal of Project Management* 22:351–58.

Garvin, D. A. 1993. Building a learning organisation. *Harvard Business Review*. 78–91.

Gherardi, S., D. Nicolini, and F. Odella. 1998. Toward a social understanding of how people learn in organizations. *Management Learning* 29:273–97.

Gibbons, M., C. Limoges, H. Nowotny, S. Schwartzman, P. Scott, and M. Trow. 1994. *The new production of knowledge: The dynamics of science and research in contemporary societies*. London: Sage Publications.

Gibson, L., and S. Pfautz. 1999. Re-engineering IT project management in an R&D organization – A case study. In *Managing business by projects*, ed. K. A. Artto, K. Kahkonen, and K. Koskinen, 86–97. Helsinki, Finland: Project Management Association.

Glanville, J. 2003. The key factors in project review. Paper given at Project Challenge 2003: Strategies for successful project delivery. Hook, Hants, UK: Management Events Ltd 2003.

Glass, R. L. 1998. *Computing calamaties: Lessons learned from products, projects and companies that failed*. Upper Saddle River, NJ: Prentice Hall.

Graham, A. K. 2000. Beyond PM 101: Lessons for managing large development programs. *Project Management Journal* 31:7–19.

Gulliver, F. R. 1987. Post-project appraisals pay. *Harvard Business Review*. March-April 65:128–31.

Hall, J., and J. Sapsed. 2005. Influences of knowledge sharing and hoarding in project-based firms. In *Knowledge management in project environments*, ed. P. Love, Z. Irani, and P. Fong. Oxford: Elsevier / Butterworth-Heinemann 57–80.

Hansen, M. T., N. Norhia, and T. Tierney. 1999. What's your strategy for managing knowledge? *Harvard Business Review*. 77:106–236.

Harris, L. 2002. The learning organisation – Myth or reality? Examples from the UK retail banking industry. *The Learning Organization* 9:78–88.

Hobday, M. 2000. The project-based organisation: An ideal form for managing complex products or systems? *Research Policy* 29:871–93.

Hodgson, D. 2002. Disciplining the professional: The case of project management. *Journal of Management Studies* 39:803–21.

Hoffman, E. J. 2003. NASA reduces uncertainty and minimizes risks with project methods. *PM Network* 6:20.

Holt, G. D., P. E. D. Love, and H. Li. 2000. The learning organisation: Towards a paradigm for mutually beneficial strategic construction alliances. *International Journal of Project Management* 18:415–22.

Huber, G. 1999. Facilitating project team learning and contributions to organizational knowledge. *Creativity and Innovation Management* 8:70–76.

Huber, G. P. 1991. Organizational learning: The contributing processes and the literatures. *Organization Science* 2:88–115.

Isabella, L. A. 1990. Evolving interpretations as a change unfolds: How managers construe key organizational events. *Academy of Management Journal* 33:7–41.

Ivory, C., N. Alderman, I. McLoughlin, R. Vaughan, and A. Thwaites. 2004. Sense-making as a process within complex service-led projects. Paper presented at the IRNOP VI: Sixth International Conference of the International Research Network of Organizing by Projects, Turku, Finland.

Johanessen, J.-A., J. Olaisen, and B. Olsen. 1999. Systemic thinking as the philosophical foundation for knowledge management and organizational learning. *Kybernetes* 28:24–46.

Johnson, B., E. Lorenz, and B.-A. Lundvall. 2002. Why all this fuss about codified and tacit knowledge? *Industrial and Corporate Change* 11:245–62.

Kalantjakos, N. J. 2001. Understanding organizational project management maturity. *Proceedings of the PMI Seminars and Symposium 2001*, CD-ROM. Newtown Square, PA: Project Management Institute.

Kamara, J. M., C. J. Anumba, and P. M. Carrilo. 2002. A CLEVER approach to selecting a knowledge management strategy. *International Journal of Project Management* 20:205–12.

Karni, R., and R. Gordon. 2000. Knowledge management in a project-oriented environment. *Proceedings of PMI Europe 2000*. Newtown Square, PA: Project Management Institute 2000.

Kasvi, J. J. J., M. Vartiainen, and M. Hailikari. 2003. Managing knowledge and knowledge competencies in projects and project organisations. *International Journal of Project Management* 21:571–82.

Keegan, A., and J. R. Turner. 2001. Quantity versus quality in project-based learning practices. *Management Learning* 32:77–98.

Kerth, N. 2000. The ritual of retrospectives. *Software Testing & Quality Engineering*. Sept-Oct 2000:53–58.

Kerzner, H. 2000. *Applied project management: Best practices on implementation*. New York: Wiley.

Kidd, J. B. 1998. Knowledge creation in Japanese manufacturing companies in Italy. *Management Learning* 29:131–46.

Kim, D. H. 1993. The link between individual and organizational learning. *Sloan Management Review* 35:37–50.

Kofman, F., and P. M. Senge. 1993. Communities of commitment: The heart of learning organizations. *Organizational Dynamics* 22:5–23.

Koskinen, K. U. 2004. Knowledge management to improve project communication and implementation. *Project Management Journal* 35:13–19.

Koskinen, K. U. 2005. Storytelling as an addition to a project-based company's organisational memory. *Proceedings of the EURAM conference*. Brussels: EURAM 2005.

Koskinen, K. U., P. Pihlanto, and H. Vanharanta. 2003. Tacit knowledge acquisition and sharing in a project work context. *International Journal of Project Management* 21:281–90.

Kotnour, T. 1999. A learning framework for project management. *Project Management Journal* 30:32–38.

Kotnour, T. 2000. Organizational learning practices in the project management environment. *International Journal of Quality and Reliability Management* 17:393–406.

Kotnour, T., and M. Hjelm. 2002. Leadership mechanisms for enabling learning within project teams. *Proceedings of OKLC 2002: The Third European Conference on Organizational Knowledge, Learning and Capabilities, Session 7-2,* Athens, Greece. Athens, Greece: Athens Laboratory of Business Administration.

Kransdorff, A. 1996. Using the benefits of hindsight – The role of post-project analysis. *The Learning Organization* 3:11–15.

Kumar, S., and D. Terpstra. 2004. The post mortem of a complex product development – Lessons learned. *Technovation* 24:805–18.

Landes, D., K. Schneider, and F. Houdek. 1999. Organizational learning and experience documentation in industrial software projects. *International Journal of Human-Computer Studies* 51:643–61.

Lave, J., and E. Wenger. 1991. *Situated learning. Legitimate peripheral participation*. Cambridge: Cambridge University Press.

Lesser, E., M. Fontaine, and J. Slusher, eds. 2000. *Knowledge and communities*. Woburn, MA: Butterworth-Heinemann.

Lesser, E., and L. Prusak. 2000. The role of communities of practice in the processes of creating, sharing and applying organizational knowledge. In *Knowledge and communities*, ed. E. Lesser, M. Fontaine, and J. Slusher. Woburn, MA: Butterworth-Heinemann.

Levene, R. J., and P. C. Gale. 2000. Organizational learning and dysfunctional project processes. *Proceedings of the PMI Seminars and Symposium 2000*, CD-ROM. Newtown Square, PA: Project Management Institute.

Liebowitz, J. 2005. Conceptualizing and implementing knowledge management. In *Knowledge management in project environments*, ed. P. Love, Z. Irani, and P. Fong. Oxford: Elsevier / Butterworth-Heinemann 1–18.

Liebowitz, J., and I. Megbolugbe. 2003. A set of frameworks to aid the project manager in conceptualizing and implementing knowledge management initiatives. *International Journal of Project Management* 21:189–98.

Lilly, B., and T. Porter. 2003. Improvement reviews in new product development. *R & D Management* 33:285–296.

Lindqvist, L., J. Söderlund, and C. Frohm. 2002. Knowledge management in technology- and project-based firms. *Proceedings of IRNOP V: Fifth International Conference of the International Research Network of Organizing by Projects.* East Horsley, UK: EuroProjex Ltd.

Linehan, C., and D. Kavanagh. 2004. From project ontologies to communities of virtue. Paper presented at the 2nd International Workshop, "Making projects critical." Bristol, UK: University of the West of England 2004.

Lipshitz, R., M. Popper, and V. Friedman. 2002. A multifacet model of organizational learning. *Journal of Applied Behavioral Science* 38:78–98.

Lipshitz, R., M. Popper, and S. Oz. 1996. Building learning organizations: The design and implementation of organizational learning mechanisms. *Journal of Applied Behavioral Science* 32:292.

Liu, A. M. M., and A. Walker. 1998. Evaluation of project outcomes. *Construction Management and Economics* 16:209–219.

Loo, R. 2002. Journaling: A learning tool for project management training and team-building. *Project Management Journal* 33:61–66.

Lyneis, J. M., K. G. Cooper, and S. A. Els. 2001. Strategic management of complex projects: A case study using system dynamics. *System Dynamics Review* 17:237–60.

Lynn, G. S., R. R. Reilly, and A. E. Akgun. 2000. Knowledge management in new product teams: Practices and outcomes. *IEEE Transactions on Engineering Management* 47:221–31.

Lytras, M. D., and A. Pouloudi. 2003. Project management as a knowledge primer: The learning infrastructure in knowledge-intensive oganizations: Projects as knowledge transformations and beyond. *The Learning Organization* 10:237–50.

MacMaster, G. 2000. Can we learn from project histories? *PM Network* 7:66–67.

Matusik, S. F., and C. W. L. Hill. 1998. The utilization of contingent work, knowledge creation, and competitive advantage. *Academy of Management: The Academy of Management Review* 23:680–97.

McDermott, R. 1999. Why information technology inspired but cannot deliver knowledge management. *California Management Review* 41:103–17.

McKenna, S. 1999. Learning through complexity. *Management Learning* 30:301–20.

Menke, M. M. 1997. Managing R&D for competitive advantage. *Research: Technology Management.* vol 45.

Middleton, C. J. 1967. How to set up a project organization. *Harvard Business Review* March-April:73–82.

Mitev, N. N. 1998. Book reviews. *Management Learning* 29:237–41.

Morecroft, J. 2004. Mental models and learning in system dynamics practice. In *Systems modelling: Theory and practice*, ed. M. Pidd. Chichester, UK: Wiley 101–26.

Moreland, R. L., and L. K. R. Argote. 1998. Training people to work in groups. In *Theory and research on small groups: Social psychological applications to social issues*, ed. R. S. Tindale, L. Heath, J. Edwards, E. J. Posavac, F. B. Bryant, J. Myers, Y. Suarez-Balcazar, and E. Henderson-King, 37–60. New York: Plenum Press.

Morris, P. W. G. 2002. Managing project management knowledge for organizational effectiveness. *Proceedings of the PMI Research Conference 2002*, 77–87. Newtown Square, PA: Project Management Institute.

Morris, P. W. G., and I. C. A. Loch. 2003. Organisational learning and knowledge creation interfaces in project-based organisations. *Proceedings of the EURAM conference*. Brussels: EURAM 2003.

Morris, P. W. G. and I. C. A. Loch. 2004a. Knowledge creation and dissemination (organizational learning) in project-based organisations. *Proceedings of the PMI Research Conference 2004*, CD-ROM. Newtown Square, PA: Project Management Institute.

Morris, P. W. G., and I. C. A. Loch. 2004b. The role of knowledge creation and dissemination in managing risk in projects. *Proceedings of the EURAM conference*. Brussels: EURAM 2004.

Morris, P. W. G., M. B. Patel, and S. H. Wearne. 2000. Research into revising the APM project management body of knowledge. *International Journal of Project Management* 18:155–64.

Mumford, A. 1994. Four approaches to learning from experience. *The Learning Organization* 1:4–10.

Nair, K. U. 2001. Adaption to creation: Progress of organizational learning and increasing complexity of learning systems. *Systems Research and Behavioral Science* 18:505–21.

Naot, Y. B.-H. L. R., and M. Popper. 2004. Discerning the quality of organizational learning. *Management Learning* 35:451–72.

NASA. See National Aeronautics and Space Administration.

National Aeronautics and Space Administration (NASA). 2004. ASK: Academy sharing knowledge (database).

Neale, C. W., and D. E. A. Holmes. 1990. Post-auditing capital projects. *Long Range Planning* 23:88–96.

Neale, C. W., and S. Letza. 1996. Improving the quality of project appraisal and management: An exercise in organizational learning. *The Learning Organization* 3:26–30.

Nevis, E. C., A. J. DiBella, and J. M. Gould. 1995. Understanding organizations as learning systems. *Sloan Management Review* 36:73–85.

Newcombe, R. 2000. The anatomy of two projects: A comparative analysis approach. *International Journal of Project Management* 18:189–99.

Newell, S. 2004. Enhancing cross-project learning. *Engineering Management Journal* 16:12–20.

Newell, S., and J. Huang. 2005. Knowledge integration processes and dynamics within the context of cross-functional projects. In *Knowledge management in project environments*, ed. P. Love, Z. Irani, and P. Fong. Oxford: Elsevier / Butterworth-Heinemann 19–40.

Nobeoka, K. 1995. Inter-project learning in new project development. *Academy of Management Best Papers Proceedings*. Briarcliff Manor, NY: Academy of Management August 1995:432–36.

Nocker, M. O. 2004. Projects as emergent space: Shifting boundaries of a multiple horizon. Paper presented at the 2nd International Workshop, "Making Projects Critical." Bristol, UK: University of the West of England 2004.

Nonaka, I. 1991. The knowledge-creating company. *Harvard Business Review* Nov-Dec:96–104.

Nonaka, I., and H. Takeuchi. 1995. *The knowledge-creating company: How Japanese companies create the dynamics of innovation*. Oxford: Oxford University Press.

O'Dell, C., and C. Jackson Grayson. 1998. *If only we knew what we know*. London: Simon and Schuster.

Office of Government Commerce. 2002. *Managing successful projects with PRINCE2 (PRINCE Guidance)*. London: The Stationery Office Books.

Orr, J. E. 1990. Sharing knowledge, celebrating identity: Common memory in a service culture. In *Collective remembering*, ed. D. Middleton and D. Edwards, 169–89. London: Sage Publications.

Oshri, I. 2000. Managing knowledge in a multiple-project environment: Communities of practice and practices in communities. *Proceedings of PMI Europe 2000 Conference* London, UK. Upper Darby, PA: Project Management Institute.

Örtenblad, A. 2002. A typology of the idea of learning organization. *Management Learning* 33:213–230.

Osterloh, M., and B. S. Frey. 2000. Motivation, knowledge transfer, and organizational forms. *Organization Science* 11:538–50.

Ottmann, R. 2000. Project benchmarking PBM: Analysis of best practices in project management. *Proceedings of the IPMA World Congress*. London, May 2000.

Packendorff, J. 1995. Inquiring into the temporary organization: New directions for project management research. *Scandanavian Journal of Management* 11:319–33.

Pan, G. S. C., and D. Flynn. 2003. Gaining knowledge from post-mortem analyses to eliminate electronic commerce project abandonment. In *E-commerce and cultural values*, ed. T. Thanasankit, 108–23. Idea Group Publishing.

Patriotta, G. 2003. *Organizational knowledge in the making: How firms create, use and institutionalise knowledge*. Oxford: Oxford University Press.

Paté-Cornell, M. E., and R. Dillon. 2001. Success factors and future challenges in the management of faster-better-cheaper projects: Lessons learned from NASA. *IEEE Transactions on Engineering Management* 48:25–35.

Pinto, J. K. 1999. Managing information systems projects: Regaining control of a runaway train. In *Managing business by projects*, ed. K. A. Artto, K. Kähkönen, and K. Koskinen, 30–43 Helsinki: Project Management Association Finland and NORDNET, Helsinki, Finland.

Pitagorsky, G. 2000. Lessons learned through process thinking and review. *PM Network* 3:35–38.

Polanyi, M. 1962. *The tacit dimension*. New York: Doubleday.

Polkinghorne, D. E. 1988. *Narrative knowing and the human sciences*. Albany, NY: State University of New York Press.

Popper, M., and R. Lipshitz. 1998. Organizational learning mechanisms: A structured and cultural approach to organizational learning. *Journal of Applied Behavioral Science* 34:161–79.

Prencipe, A., and F. Tell. 2001. Inter-project learning: processes and outcomes of knowledge codification in project-based firms. *Research Policy* 30:1373–94.

Prichard, C., R. Hull, M. Chumer, and H. Willmott, eds. 2000. *Managing knowledge: Critical investigations of work and learning*. Basingstoke, UK: Macmillan.

Project Management Institute. 2000. *A guide to the project management book of knowledge (PMBOK® guide)*. Newtown Square, PA: Project Management Institute.

Project Management Institute. 2004. *Organizational project management maturity model (OPM3®)*. Newtown Square, PA: Project Management Institute.

Purser, R. E., W. A. Pasmore, and R. V. Tenkasi. 1992. The influence of deliberations on learning in new product development teams. *Journal of Engineering and Technology Management* 9:1–28.

Raelin, J. A. 2001. Public reflection as the basis for learning. *Management Learning* 32:11–30.

Ramaprasad, A., and A. N. Prakash. 2003. Emergent project management: How foreign managers can leverage local knowledge. *International Journal of Project Management* 21:198–205.

Rasper, V., M. Stanier, and P. Carluccio. 2002. A real life approach to lessons learned. *Proceedings of the PMI Seminars and Symposium 2002*, CD-ROM. Newtown Square, PA: Project Management Institute.

Reger, G., and D. von Wichert-Nick. 1997. A learning organization for R&D management. *International Journal of Technology Management* 13:796–817.

Reich, B. H., and S. Y. Wee. 2004. Searching for knowledge management practices in the PMBOK Guide. *Proceedings of the PMI Research Conference 2004*, CD-ROM. Newtown Square, PA: Project Management Institute.

Rigano, D., and J. Edwards. 1998. Incorporating reflection into work practice: A case study. *Management Learning* 29:431–446.

Risk Management Research and Development Program Collaboration. 2002. RMRP-2002-02, Version 1.0, Risk Management Research and Development Program Collaboration [Formal Collaboration: INCOSE Risk Management Working Group; Project Management Institute Risk Management Specific Interest Group; UK Association for Project Management Risk Specific Interest Group].

Robinson, H. S., P. M. Carrillo, C. J. Anumba, and A. M. Al-Ghassani. 2004. Developing a business case for knowledge management: The IMPaKT approach. *Construction Management and Economics* 22:733–43.

Roth, G., and Kleiner, A. 1998. Developing organizational memory through learning histories.

Organisational Dynamics. Autumn 1998 27:43–59.

Ruggles, R. 1998. The state of the notion: Knowledge management in practice. *California Management Review* 40:80–89.

Scarbrough, H., M. Bresnen, L. F. Edelman, S. Laurent, S. Newell, and J. Swan. 2004. The process of project-based learning: An exploratory study. *Management Learning* 35:491–506.

Scarbrough, H., J. Swan, and J. Preston. 1999. *Knowledge management: A literature review.* London: Institute of Personnel and Development.

Scarbrough, H., S. Laurent, M. Bresnen, L. Edelman, and S, Newell. 2004. Project-based learning and the role of learning boundaries. *Organization Studies* 25:1579–1600.

Schindler, M., and M. Eppler. 2003. Harvesting project knowledge: A review of project learning methods and success factors. *International Journal of Project Management* 21:219–28.

Schlichter, J. 2001. PMI's organizational project management maturity model: Emerging standards. *Proceedings of the PMI Seminars and Symposium 2001,* CD-ROM. Newtown Square, PA: Project Management Institute.

Schoeniger, E. 2005. Message relay. *Leadership in Project Management Annual* 2005.

Schofield, J., and D. C. Wilson. 1995. The role of capital investment project reams in organisational learning. *Scandanavian Journal of Management* 11:423–36.

Schulz, M. 2001. The uncertain relevance of newness: Organizational learning and knowledge flows. *Academy of Management Journal* 44:661–81.

Schwandt, D. R., and M. J. Marquardt. 2000. *Organizational learning: From world-class theories to global best practices.* Washington, DC: George Washington University, Centre for the Study of Learning.

Schön, D. 1991. *The reflective practitioner.* Aldershot, UK: Ashgate Publishing Ltd.

Senge, P. M. 1990. *The fifth discipline.* New York: Doubleday.

Senge, P. M., A. Kleiner, C. Roberts, R. Ross, and B. Smith. 1994. *The fifth discipline fieldbook: Strategies and tools for building a learning organisation.* New York: Doubleday.

Sense, A. J. 2002. Project teams as learning entities. *Proceedings of the PMI Research Conference 2002,* 457–65. Newtown Square, PA: Project Management Institute.

Sense, A. J. 2003a. Learning generators: Project teams re-conceptualized. *Project Management Journal* 34:4–11.

Sense, A. J. 2003b. A model of the politics of project leader learning. *International Journal of Project Management* 21:107–14.

Sense, A. J., and M. Antoni. 2003. Exploring the politics of project learning. *International Journal of Project Management* 21:487–94.

Simon, H. A. 1991. Bounded rationality and organizational learning. *Organization Science* 2:125–34.

Smith, P. A. C. 2001. Action learning and reflective practice in project environments that are related to leadership development. *Management Learning* 32:31–48.

Solomon, C. M. 1994. HR facilitates the learning organization concept. *Personnel Journal* 73:56–65.

Spender, J.-C. 1996. Organizational knowledge, learning and memory: Three concepts in search of a theory. *Journal of Organizational Change Management* 9:63–78.

Stacey, R. D. 2001. Mainstream thinking about learning and knowledge creation in organizations. In *Complex responsive processes in organizations: Learning and knowledge creation*, ed. R. D. Stacey, D. Griffin, and P. Shaw, 33–37. Routledge.

Starbuck, W. H. 1992. Learning by knowledge-intensive firms. *Journal of Management Studies* 19:1–27.

Starkey, K., and P. Madan. 2001. Bridging the relevance gap: Aligning stakeholders in the future of management research. *British Journal of Management* 12:S3–S26.

Steichen, K. A. 2001. Project management communities of practice – Advancing the practice. *Proceedings of the PMI Seminars and Symposium 2001*, CD-ROM. Newtown Square, PA: Project Management Institute.

Stein, E. W., and V. Zwass. 1995. Actualizing organizational memory with information systems. *Information Systems Research* 6:85–117.

Stephens, C. H., J. Kasher, A. Welsh, and J. Plaskoff. 1999. How to transfer innovations, solutions, and lessons learned across product teams: Implementation of a knowledge management system. *Proceedings of the PMI Seminars and Symposium 1999*. Newtown Square, PA: Project Management Institute.

Sterman, J. D. 2000. *Business dynamics: Systems thinking and modeling for a complex world*. Boston: McGraw-Hill Higher Education.

Stevens, M. 2002. *Project management pathways*. High Wycombe, UK: Association for Project Management.

Storey, J., and B. Barnett. 2000. Knowledge management initiatives: Learning from failure. *Journal of Knowledge Management* 4:145–56.

Strang, K. D. 2003. Organizational learning across projects. *Proceedings of the PMI Global Congress 2003—North America*, CD-ROM. Newtown Square, PA: Project Management Institute.

Styhre, A., P.-E. Josephson, and I. Knauseder. 2004. Learning capabilities in organizational networks: Case studies of six construction projects. *Construction Management and Economics* 22:957–66.

Swan, J., H. Scarbrough, and M. Robertson. 2002. The construction of 'communities of practice' in the management of innovation. *Management Learning* 33:477–96.

Szulanski, G. 1996. Exploring internal stickiness: Impediments to the transfer of best practice within the firm. *Strategic Management Journal* 17:27–43.

Tacla, C. A., and J.-P. Barth s. 2003. A multi-agent system for acquiring and sharing lessons learned. *Computers in Industry* 52:5–16.

Terrell, M. S. 1999. Implementing a lessons learned process that works. *Proceedings of the PMI Seminars and Symposium 1999*. Newtown Square, PA: Project Management Institute.

Texas Department of Information Resources. 2000. Process for post project reviews. *Quality assurance guidelines for projects in Texas State agencies*. Austin, TX: Texas Department of Information Resources 2000.

Themistocleous, G., and S. H. Wearne. 2000. Project Management topic coverage in journals. *International Journal of Project Management* 18:7–11.

Toft, B. 1992. The failure of hindsight. *Disaster Prevention and Management: An International Journal* 1:48–61.

Tsoukas, H., and M. J. Hatch. 2001. Complex thinking, complex practice: The case for a narrative approach to organizational complexity. *Human Relations* 54:979–1013.

Turner, J. R., A. Keegan, and L. Crawford. 2000. Learning by experience in the project-based organisation. *Proceedings of the PMI Research Conference 2004*, CD-ROM. Newtown Square, PA: Project Management Institute.

Vaughan, D. 1996. *The Challenger launch decision. Risky technology, Culture and Deviance at NASA.* Chicago: University of Chicago Press.

Venugopal, V., and W. Baets. 1995. Intelligent support systems for organizational learning. *The Learning Organization* 2:22–34.

Vera, D., and M. Crossan. 2003. Organizational learning and knowledge management: Toward an integrative framework. In *The Blackwell Handbook of Organizational Learning and Knowledge Mangement,*, ed. M. A. Lyles and M. Easterby-Smith, 122–142. Oxford: Blackwell Publishing.

von Glasersfeld, E. 1995. *Radical constructivism: A way of knowing and learning.* London: Routledge Falmer.

von Krogh, G. 1998. Care in knowledge creation. *California Management Review* 40:133–53.

von Krogh, G., and S. Grand. 1999. Justification in knowledge creation: Dominant logic in management discourses. In *Knowledge creation: A source of value,* ed. G. von Krogh, I. Nonaka, and T. Nishiguchi, 13–35. London: Palgrave Macmillan.

von Krogh, G., J. Roos, and D. Kleine. 1998. *Knowing in firms: Understanding, managing and measuring knowledge.* London: Sage Publications.

von Zedtwitz, M. 2002. Organizational learning through post-project reviews in R & D. *R & D Management* 32:255–68.

Wateridge, J. 2002. (Post) Project Evaluation Review. In *Project management pathways*, 65-1 to 65-12. Association for Project Management. High Wycombe, UK: Association for Project Management Ltd.

Weiser, M., and J. Morrison. 1998. Project memory: Information management for project teams. *Journal of Management Information Systems* 14:149–66.

Wenger, E. 1998. *Communities of practice: Learning, meaning and identity.* Cambridge, UK: Cambridge University Press.

Wheelwright, S.C., and K. B. Clark. 1992. Revolutionizing product development: Quantum leaps in speed, efficiency and quality. New York: The Free Press.

Wilkins, A. L. 1984. The creation of company cultures: the role of stories in human resource systems. *Human Resource Management* 23:41–60.

Williams, T. 2004. Learning the hard lessons from projects easily. *International Journal of Project Management* 22:273–79.

Williams, T. 2005. Assessing and building on project management theory in the light of badly over-run projects. *IEEE Transactions in Engineering Management* 52:497–508.

Williams, T., F. Ackermann, and C. Eden. 2003. Structuring a delay and disruption claim: An application of cause-mapping and system dynamics. *European Journal of Operational Research* 148:192–204.

Williams, T., F. Ackermann, C. Eden, and S. Howick. 2005. Learning from project failure. In *Knowledge management in project environments*, ed. P. Love, Z. Irani, and P. Fong, 219–35. Oxford: Elsevier / Butterworth-Heinemann.

Williams, T., C. Eden, F. Ackermann, S. Howick, V. Bergamini, A. Daley, and K. Gill. 2001. The use of project post-mortems. *Proceedings of the PMI Seminars and Symposium 2001*, CD-ROM. Newtown Square, PA: Project Management Institute.

Williams, T., C. Eden, F. Ackermann, and A. Tait. 1995. The effects of design changes and delays on project costs. *Journal of the Operational Research Society* 46:809–18.

Williams, T., C. Eden, F. Ackermann, and A. Tait. 1995. Vicious circles of parallelism. *International Journal of Project Management* 13:151–55.

Williams, T. M. 1999. The need for new paradigms for complex projects. *International Journal of Project Management* 17:269–273.

Williams, T. M. 2003. Learning from projects [abstract]. *Journal of the Operational Research Society* 54:443–451.

Winch, G. 1998. The growth of self-employment in British construction. *Construction Management and Economics* 16:531–42.

Winter, M., and J. Thomas. 2004. Understanding the lived experience of managing projects: The need for more emphasis on the practice of managing. *Proceedings of the PMI Research Conference 2004*, CD-ROM. Newtown Square, PA: Project Management Institute.

Wreme, E., and S. Sorrenti. 1997. Using systems thinking tools to help Australian managers increase their capacity for perception. *The Learning Organization* 4:180–87.

Zollo, M., and S. G. Winter. 2002. Deliberate learning and the evolution of dynamic capabilities. *Organization Science* 13:339–51.